GW00734188

Managing
School Development

A Practical Guide

Managing
School Development
A Practical Guide

Mel West & Mel Ainscow
Cambridge Institute of Education

David Fulton Publishers
London

David Fulton Publishers Ltd
2 Barbon Close, London WC1N 3JX

First published in Great Britain by
David Fulton Publishers, 1991

Note: The right of Mel West and Mel Ainscow to be identified as authors of this work has been asserted by them in accordance with the Copyright, Designs and Patents Act 1988.

Copyright © Mel West and Mel Ainscow

British Library Cataloguing in Publication Data

West, Mel
 Managing school development: a practical guide.
 1. Schools. Management
 I. Title   II. Ainscow, Mel
 371.2

 ISBN 1-85346-144-X

All rights reserved. No part of this publication may be reproduced, stored in a retrieval system or transmitted, in any form, or by any means, electronic, mechanical, photocopying, recording or otherwise, without the prior permission of the publishers.

Typeset by Chapterhouse, Formby
Printed in Great Britain by
BPCC Wheatons Ltd, Exeter

Contents

Preface

The main concern of this book is with effective school management. It has been written at a time when changes in legislation have placed new demands on those who work in schools, demands which make it particularly important that planning at the school level is managed successfully.

Broadly stated the aims of the book are:

● to explain the management challenges that schools face
● to suggest positive ways of engaging with these challenges.

Our intended audience includes, therefore, all those concerned with improving the effectiveness of schools. Specifically we have in mind headteachers and others with management tasks in schools; members of the advisory and administrative staff of local education authorities, and school governors.

We have characterised the book as 'a practical guide'. Our intention has been to provide an easy-to-read, accessible text that allows busy people to engage with key issues, reflect upon relevant ideas and learn about specific techniques. We have also provided details of sources of further information for those readers who wish to pursue particular topics in greater detail.

The book is organised in two parts. In Part One we consider the changing context in which schools have to operate, drawing out the management implications. This analysis leads us to summarise some ideas about possible management responses. Part Two consists of a compendium of practical approaches with particular respect to the processes of reviewing, planning and implementing school policies.

The arguments and suggestions made in this book are our own and, consequently, we take responsibility for them. However we must acknowledge the contribution of many others. In particular we are aware of the influence of the many teachers, advisers and LEA officers with whom we have contact. Our thinking has also been stimulated by discussions with our colleagues at the Cambridge Institute of Education.

Finally we must thank Caroline Bean who has shown endless patience in typing and retyping the text.

MEL WEST
MEL AINSCOW
Cambridge, September 1990

PART ONE

Managing School Development: Contexts and Concepts

The 1990s are challenging times for those who have management roles in schools. Debates in the community about the purposes of schooling and concern about standards in education have increased pressure on those responsible for the running of schools during times of rapid change in curriculum content and process. In Britain recent legislation has further focused attention on the way in which the education service operates.

The first section of this book considers the significance of current developments for the management of schools.

In the first chapter we provide an analysis of the new context in which school managers will have to operate. In particular we draw attention to two apparently contradictory trends. These are:

(1) The move towards greater centralisation of decision-making within the education service (i.e. **prescription**); and
(2) The increased emphasis on schools having greater autonomy about their use of resources (i.e. **devolution**).

Having explored the nature of these trends we then go on to outline their implications, and identify a series of challenges to which schools will need to respond if they are to survive in the difficult years ahead.

The second chapter considers specific management skills which can assist schools during this period of change. It provides a framework for thinking about management theory and research from non-educational settings which seem to have something to offer school managers at this crucial time in the development of school management structures and practices.

The third chapter acknowledges that whilst 'importing' such ideas and approaches is both appropriate and inevitable, the specific application of

1

management tools within the school needs to reflect educational values beliefs and objectives. It develops a model illustrating the relationships between educational and managerial purposes, and underlines the need to establish criteria to assess educational (effectiveness) and managerial (efficiency) outcomes. Recognising that the knowledge and experience required to make judgements which are educationally sound is widely distributed amongst teachers at all levels within schools, it suggests that attempts to draw as many teachers as possible into the management process of the school, via delegation and empowerment, is a priority for school management teams.

CHAPTER ONE

A New Context for School Managers

The Education Reform Act (1988) has significantly altered the context in which schools operate. The relationship between Local Education Authorities (LEAs) and their schools has been dramatically changed by the legislation, as the head-teacher's role has changed in emphasis from administrative to managerial. This shift, most frequently referred to as LMS – the 'Local Management of Schools' (see Coopers and Lybrand, 1988) – brings with it a number of new challenges for school managers, and underlines several old ones which have perhaps had less attention in the past than was desirable. The full impact of these changes will, inevitably, take a number of years to feed through the system. What is clear is that school governors and head-teachers will be required to think and to act in new ways, as the major responsibility for the management of the school transfers away from the local education authority and into the (often several hundred) separate establishments which it comprises. Self-determination will be not simply a right, but make a crucial contribution to school policies and their success or failure.

Simultaneously however, a different part of the Act requires schools to implement the National Curriculum proposals, together with the attendant assessment and testing procedures. Schools then are confronted by two immediate, and possibly in some aspects contradictory, requirements: to demonstrate that they are responding to a rationally determined curriculum pattern; and to ensure that they are making the best possible local decisions about policies, priorities and resources. These two features of the new educational landscape, the **prescription** of what schools should be providing for pupils and the **devolution** of decisions about how such provision can be made to governors and head-teachers, need to be considered very carefully by school managers. Both have important implications for management structures and practices within the school.

4

Responding to prescription

The introduction of the National Curriculum constitutes a radical shift in curriculum content and structure for many schools. More fundamentally it can be seen as a major change in both how, and by whom, decisions about curriculum content and structure are made. The tradition established through the 1960s and 1970s has been one in which these decisions were very heavily influenced by teachers. Indeed for many of the senior staff currently managing schools career development and curriculum development have been inextricably linked. The challenges posed by a central curriculum model should, therefore, not be under-estimated. They throw up a number of important areas in which schools need to make a response. These will include:

- management of time
- teacher competencies and skills
- classroom process
- teacher morale and motivation
- monitoring school policy
- measurement of school performance

Let us consider each of these in turn.

(i) *Management of time*

The work of any school is essentially about the use of time, staff time and pupil time. The National Curriculum, though not conceived as a curricular pattern which would occupy 100 per cent of pupil time, seems in practice to require more than 100 per cent if it is all to be squeezed in. Already, for example, some schools have investigated the possibility of 'twilight' classes to make a second language available, and at least one LEA has considered whether and how teachers could be paid for offering such classes. Implementing the National Curriculum therefore stretches the already crowded pupil day to bursting point. Similar difficulties will arise for teachers: difficulties which are compounded by the pressures created by other changes, and underwritten by school budgets which often would appear to require a reduction in either the numbers of teachers employed or the average level of experience of the staff, if they are not to be exceeded.

(ii) *Teacher competencies and skills*

Not unnaturally, schools tend to recruit staff whose patterns of knowledge and skills coincide with the school's own curriculum priorities. In this context the notion of curricular balance is one which varies enormously from school to school according to such factors as the values of individual head-teachers and their staffs, the difficulty of recruiting staff in particular curricular areas, the preferences of governors and of parents and the availability of resources. A further problem arises from the segmented structure of many schools, whether vertical (subject based) or horizontal (age-cohort related), which has made promotion more difficult for the 'non-specialist' to achieve. It is clear that, as the requirements of the National Curriculum have been spelt out, more and more schools have to face up to a discrepancy between the required pattern of teacher knowledge and skills and the actual knowledge and skills available within the current staff of the school.

(iii) *Classroom process*

The present sweep of curriculum change – and this encompasses not just the National Curriculum but also other important curriculum development initiatives, such as the Technical and Vocational Education Initiative (TVEI) – brings with it significant pressure for changes in classroom practice. Not only is the teacher's knowledge base questioned by the drawing up of a National Curriculum content plan, but at the same time teachers are being asked to develop new classroom strategies and new methods of working with pupils. Unless handled very carefully and sensitively, this could become a tremendously de-skilling experience for teachers; one which is likely at best to reduce teacher enthusiasm and commitment in the short term, at worst likely to reduce teacher competence in the long term. There is an urgent need, therefore, to evolve new ways of thinking about pupil–teacher relationships and interactions, and to assist teachers in the development of skills appropriate to supporting these processes.

(iv) *Teacher morale and motivation*

The de-skilling nature of these changes, combined with time pressures and the external origins of the change, could well contribute to a further problem for school managers – that of teacher morale. The difficulty of creating within the school a climate which is supportive to curricular changes that have been determined outside the school is well charted. Bolam (1984), reviewing the available research findings on the promotion of curriculum change, has underlined the importance of teacher involvement and teacher influence:

> ...it should involve adaptive and continuing planning by the major participants and interest groups involved, giving opportunity to adapt the goals and content of the innovation and providing mechanisms for feedback on progress; ...
>
> people in key leadership roles (for example, heads, advisers and chief education officers) should be overtly supportive and participate directly when appropriate; ...
>
> there should be opportunities for members of the target user group to develop and modify the innovation locally by adapting the materials and by learning about the innovation's characteristics and developing a sense of 'owning' it; ...

The National Curriculum starts, then, with a number of obstacles to overcome and the method of its introduction will be a key factor to successful implementation.

Further, many teachers are bewildered by the sheer extent of current developments and this can lead to a sense of confusion, even alienation, which leads in turn via reduced morale to reduced commitment and motivation. A particularly difficult feature of the National Curriculum is that it may well be simultaneously alienating some senior staff in schools – staff whom we look to as a source of motivation for classroom teachers. We may well be expecting poorly motivated school managers to somehow set aside their own sense of frustration and nevertheless encourage and stimulate their similarly stressed and frustrated teaching staffs. This is a daunting task, and one which will need continued support from school and from LEA if it is to be accomplished.

(v) *Monitoring school policy*

The key issue here is how the school, however proficient its curriculum planning processes have been, will ensure that what is happening in classrooms is consistent with the 'agreed' policies. Handy and Aitken (1986) have pointed out that a major feature of schools as organisations (when compared with industrial or commercial organisations) has been the extent to which they foster a multiplicity of purposes amongst teachers. Teachers have traditionally enjoyed a considerable level of classroom autonomy and schools have traditionally encouraged teachers to develop and pursue their own goals and objectives. It may well be that the need for structural reform in schools mentioned above will be further supported by a need to ensure that the management structure is able to monitor the extent to which individual teachers are implementing agreed school policies.

An example of where policy monitoring is vital relates to the increased emphasis on cross-curricular themes and dimensions. This is, in some ways, one of the most frustrating aspects of the National Curriculum, or at least the way in which it has been published. The piecemeal release of reports produced by separate and, and in some cases, single-subject working groups to some extent questions the credibility of the exercise as, one by one, foundation and core subject requirements are communicated to the school. Yet schools must make sense of these unrelated subject directives, cohere them into an overall curriculum pattern, and ensure that the cross-curricular themes and dimensions, which are implicit in the 1988 Act and are sometimes hard to locate within the Working Group reports, are also covered. This creates a significant curriculum management task within the school, one which may require radical changes in traditional approaches to school structures and organisation. They key issue here, which will be returned to later, is how far existing patterns of school organisation are capable of delivering the National Curriculum in a coherent and integrated way, ensuring that continuity and progression are maintained.

(vi) *Measurement of school performance*

A further area to which schools may need to respond involves the measuring of school performance. It has to be acknowledged that once information about pupil performance becomes available through national testing it will be looked at very closely, for example, by parents. Similarly, once the findings from current Department of Education and Science investigations into the use of 'performance indicators' are published, these can be expected to have an impact on how schools are 'ranked' within the community. If something called a Performance Indicator is available, parents will inevitably take this into account when making decisions about the schooling which will best serve their children. Thus schools will be under pressure not only to implement the National Curriculum but to demonstrate, in an increasingly competitive educational market-place, that they are doing so successfully.

Responding to devolution

Though it is the allocation of budgets to individual schools which has attracted the most publicity, the implications of financial devolution to school governors and head-teachers are much more far-reaching than the transfer of financial accountability. The Coopers and Lybrand Report (1988) points out that

> The changes require a new culture and philosophy of the organisation of education at the school level. They are more than purely financial; they need a general shift in management.

Underlining this shift, David Hill (1988), the then Local Financial Management Project Leader in Cambridgeshire, where much of the piloting of financial devolution took place, asserted that

> attitudes towards LFM have been transformed since that time. It is now perceived as local *management*, an opportunity for heads, staffs and governors to exercise greater powers of decision-making about resource allocation to the benefit of schools and pupils.

Devolution, then, is not about the transfer of a narrow financial responsibility to the school, it is about transferring the location of decisions about policies, staffing and resources. It is about the creation of a management function within the school which greatly extends the scope, range and types of decisions which schools can make for themselves. Though these decisions must still be made within the context of national and local policies, and the school remains accountable to the LEA for the consequences of decisions made, this nevertheless constitutes a major increase in managerial responsibility at school level, and as with the National Curriculum, brings with it a series of new challenges and opportunities to which schools will need to respond.

Some of these challenges will only become clear with time, but others are already apparent. These include:

- establishing school objectives
- budgetary planning
- the school as employer
- increased governor involvement
- the school in the market place.

We will consider briefly each of these areas, to draw out the management implications of the 1988 Act.

(i) *Establishing school objectives*

As mentioned above, whilst the National Curriculum Working Groups have laid down guidance for schools in the specific areas of the curriculum, how the advice of the various subject panels is integrated into a whole school curriculum pattern remains a decision for individual schools. They will therefore need to decide how best to implement the National Curriculum, and will need to develop an implementation plan which reflects the staffing and other resources available, as well as the timetable set out by the government. This will mean that each school needs to review its current provision, scrutinise national requirements, and establish its own programme for implementation. In doing so it will need to ensure that there are clear objectives, that these objectives are time and resource related, and that school effort is co-ordinated behind securing these objectives, rather than fragmented amongst departmental, subject and individual goals. This statement of objectives indicates the school's priorities and in so doing represents the school's expression of its values as well as its goals.

In this sense, the first task of the devolved school is to determine what constitutes *effective* performance, and then to consider how this can be *efficiently* pursued. This entails a clear understanding of the difference between effectiveness and efficiency, as well as the link between them. At its simplest, effectiveness is about achieving appropriate goals, i.e. 'doing the right things'. By contrast, efficiency relates not to the quality of goals, but to the way in which goals are pursued, i.e. 'doing things right'. The devolved school must find some way of uniting these two concepts. **The aim must be to manage resources efficiently towards the achievement of objectives which constitute effective educational outcomes for pupils.**

It could be argued, of course, that the National Curriculum simplifies matters for schools – that in establishing a series of curriculum targets for the school it obviates the need to think further about what is meant by effective schooling. Those who accept this will presumably see local management as a 'house-keeping' function – focusing on resource use and efficiency issues rather than addressing the more fundamental issues associated with the purposes of schooling. This may however be a dangerous approach.

Consider, for example, recent GCSE results. A review of pupils' success rates in the various subjects reveals that the most impressive pass rates have been recorded in Greek and Latin. In terms of the return on teaching effort therefore, these subjects would appear to be the most efficiently taught subjects tested at GCSE level. Unfortunately, it does not follow that schooling will be a more effective process if more pupils are taught more Greek.

Efficiency-led approaches to decision-making can then be misguided –

either because there are special factors which have contributed to the efficiency levels achieved in a particular area (such as the pre-selection that influences which pupils will have access to Greek and Latin GCSE) that will not be generally available; or because it will benefit the school little to improve its performance in those areas which add little to the pupils' learning experiences.

Each school must therefore determine its own localised definition of effectiveness. In doing so it will, of course, be influenced by the National Curriculum requirements, but it will also take account of LEA policies, the social and demographic characteristics of its catchment area, the views of governors and of parents, the strengths, weaknesses and beliefs of its staff and, above all, its diagnosis of the needs of its pupils. This is at the nub of local management, the empowerment of the school to establish objectives in partnership with its community, leading to the possibility of a responsive and locally determined series of goals for the school.

Certainly, the extent to which these goals can be realised and the costs involved in realising them will depend upon the management skills of the school's senior staff as well as the quality of its teachers. Therefore, being able to manage the school's resources efficiently is an important determinant of success, but it cannot in itself compensate for the lack of an appropriate, realistic and clearly communicated set of objectives for the school.

(ii) *Budgetary planning*

A second implication of financial devolution is the need to develop budgetary planning skills at school level. What is important here is conceiving a budget as a method of indicating the agreed levels of resourcing (human and material) necessary to secure specific objectives. A budget, then, is not a sum of money looking for projects, but a carefully compiled estimate of the resources needed for an agreed project to be carried through.

The number of projects which can be funded at any one time depends upon the total sum of money made available to the school under its own LEA's formula for the distribution of the Schools' Budget. The budgetary planning process will therefore need to reflect the real level of resourcing available to the school, but should not start from there. It should seek to identify priorities within the school's objectives and to cost the implications of pursuing particular objectives so that it is able to maximise the benefits to the school by selecting its most important objectives and funding these first, continuing to follow priorities until the total available sum is accounted for.

The possibility of virement, that is the facility to move money from one budget heading to another, means that it is important to have a clear picture of the costs and benefits associated with particular activities, and a willingness to transfer funds between activities. Though staff time is the major item of expenditure, and so needs particularly careful management, a much clearer relationship between resource use and acquisition on the one hand and the school's agreed objectives on the other needs to be forged.

A concern for many schools is that the sum of money the school receives under formula funding will be less (sometimes significantly so) than the amount which was spent on the school under previous funding arrangements. In these circumstances the task of the governors and head-teachers may be to consider which activities or areas of expenditure can be cut without significantly reducing the school's effectiveness. Sometimes the answer will be none, so that the early experience of self-management for these schools will be making difficult decisions about whether to reduce the number or the quality of objectives currently being pursued by the school.

(iii) *The school as employer*

A further implication of devolution that requires a response is the redesignation, for a number of functions, of the school rather than the LEA as employer. This brings with it a number of new responsibilities, and extends existing ones. It is, for example, necessary to develop a series of *staffing or personnel management* functions. It may well be that the tradition of encouraging staff to seek promotion elsewhere, for instance, is halted. Governors and head-teachers may by contrast become increasingly keen on internal development and the promotion of staff who are 'known' to the school. Similarly, there is now a clear incentive to the school to look at current patterns of and spending on staff development activities, and to consider whether there could be ways of overlapping school and individual needs within the staff development programme to a greater extent than has been achieved in the past.

There is also the question of compensation planning – what salary structures best serve the interests of the school and its staff, how can these be negotiated and implemented? The Interim Report on Teachers' Pay (1990) indicates increasing amounts of freedom for schools to determine pay levels for particular jobs in light of local needs and circumstances. It may well be that nationally agreed pay scales will become advisory rather than mandatory, as governors and head-teachers consider how pay levels can be managed within the context of such factors as the need to 'balance the books' or to recruit and retain staff in particular curricular areas. Similar issues will arise in relation to the contracts offered to individual staff members.

This change in relationship between governors, head-teachers and school staffs may also require a different approach to *employee relations*. The industrial relations function currently undertaken by many managers in other sectors may spread into schools. Some agreed method of evaluating jobs, for example, may be desirable, with an accompanying process of appeal available to those who feel unhappy with their own grading. A more general grievance procedure could be required within the school, though this would need to be clearly spelt out. The Education Reform Act 1988 also requires school governors to establish both the rules and procedures through which disciplinary action against teachers will be conducted.

The relationship between head-teachers and their staffs may also be affected by the devolution of the employer function to schools. Heads will become clearly and visibly *accountable to teachers* for the decisions which they take, or recommend to governors, about staffing issues. In many schools, through factors such as falling rolls and school mergers, there are staff on 'protected' posts. When such 'protection' has to be funded out of the school budget it can be anticipated that teachers will take a keen interest in the consequences of such payments for their own career or subject development. It may also, in larger schools, become increasingly difficult to justify the post of 'third deputy'. Head-teachers must expect to be questioned on these issues, by governors as well as staff, and must be prepared to justify their decisions.

(iv) *Increased governor involvement in the life of the school*

The Education Reform Act 1988, in transferring responsibility for the management of the school to its governors, completes the process of transformation of governor roles which began with the Education Act 1980 and was significantly advanced under the Education Act (No 2) 1986. Though substantial delegation of powers to head-teachers is both inevitable and appropriate, governors will nevertheless take on a much more direct role in the school's life. It is important that head-teachers develop strategies which enable this new role to be as helpful to the school as possible. Ways must be found to tap into governor expertise, and to make it available to the school; to enlist governor support for school projects; to increase governor involvement in and understanding of the processes which take place in school, so that their debates about school policy are informed, their decisions about school priorities correct. Thomas (1988), outlining the ways in which governor involvement in the management of his own school altered during the Local Financial Management pilot scheme in Cambridgeshire, concludes that a more active role for governors is beneficial to the school.

> Specialist knowledge has been developed; governors are much more aware of the life of the school, and are giving significantly more time to school matters.

He does however caution against interference in the day-to-day running of the school, suggesting that the proper focus for *governor decision-making* (as opposed to their involvement, which can be much broader) is the overall planning function.

(v) *The school in the market-place*

A further implication of devolution is the link between pupil numbers and the school budget. Though the actual amounts vary between LEAs, formula funding means that pupil numbers are by far the most important determinant of the distribution of funds to schools. There are, of course, many schools that have been operating in competitive environments for a number of years, as they have fought to hang onto their share of pupils in times of falling rolls. But this direct link, between success in recruiting pupils and funding, is new – as is the automatic reduction in funding should school numbers fall. Inevitably this places pressure on the school to become 'market-orientated', most obviously in those areas where (particularly secondary) schools have shrunk rather than closed as overall pupil numbers decreased.

This trend seems likely to extend as schools come to recognise the importance of projecting an appropriate image. However, though it may well make sense to the individual school, either because it calculates that resources used to project the school's image will pay dividends in terms of pupil numbers and therefore funding, or because it feels compelled by the promotional efforts of neighbouring schools to establish a 'presence' in the market-place, it must be remembered that it is not possible (except perhaps at 16+) to increase the size of the total market through promotional efforts. Perhaps the reluctance of many schools to engage the marketing dimension is based on the recognition that if, in five years

14

time, all schools are spending, say, even one or two per cent of their budgets on marketing and promotional activities and the distribution of pupils across schools is broadly similar to the present position, then in effect schools will have reduced the amount spent on providing educational resources. Nevertheless, the possibility of short-term gains to the individual school would seem to make competitive activities inevitable in the educational market-place which recent reforms have established.

Summary

This introductory chapter has outlined the new context in which school managers must operate. In particular it has drawn attention to the challenges that are presented as a result of the move towards a decentralisation of decision-making within the education service, and the increased emphasis on individual schools having greater control over their use of resources. This account has led us to draw attention to a range of issues that schools need to consider as they respond to challenges facing state education in the 1990s.

CHAPTER TWO

Establishing Management Principles

Confronted by the many changes referred to in the previous chapter head-teachers must find some way of re-conceptualising the school as a management structure and their own roles as managerial in nature. Coopers and Lybrand (1988) sum this up when they state:

> In short, the change at school level is from administration (of centrally determined programmes) to management (of local resources). What is required is a fundamental change in the philosophy of the organisation of education. Thus the changes required in the culture and in the management processes are much wider than purely financial and should be recognised as such.

The time available to make this adjustment is, however, short – head-teachers have to develop new patterns of management within the twin pressures of fixed budgets and increasing competition. It will be necessary to establish goals for the school from the outset, in many cases before there has been sufficient time for deliberation and consultation. Though it will be possible to alter these goals, it is important to try to get them right, since, as Fidler (1989) points out:

> ... the prime aim of all schools must be to exist in the future, and the Education Reform Act very much leaves the destiny of the school dependent on its own actions. The capacity for a school to disappear very much now lies with the school.

The highest priority then, for senior staff in schools, is to develop those skills which relate to long term or strategic management – being able to conceptualise 'the school in the future', and to communicate this vision to staff as a basis for planning and for action. This strategic management dimension is one which has been recognised as vital in industry and commerce for many years and it may be that the devolved school should look first at what can be learned from these environments.

Identifying strategic management skills

Since there is a bewildering range of management literature available it is necessary to identify the key issues before seeking help. A sensible framework would seem to be provided by considering what managers need to be able to do, irrespective of the context in which they work. From this can be developed a picture of the skills managers will most frequently need to draw upon, which can in turn be grouped into three areas of management competency (see Figure 2.1). In each of these areas there are available models, approaches, ways of thinking which, though they originate in non-educational settings, may be helpful to school managers in their new situation. Some examples of how general management thinking and writing can be brought to bear on these processes within a school setting are considered below.

Figure 2.1   Three areas of management competency

CONCEPTUAL SKILLS
These are needed in order to evolve a long term view of where the school is going. They are relevant to such activities as:

● identifying the areas in which the school needs objectives to guide its progress;
● considering how these objectives can best be evolved and expressed;
● recognising changes in circumstances which require additions or revisions to the school's objectives.

TECHNICAL SKILLS
These help school managers to devise and to implement strategies and programmes for securing school objectives and relate to:

● establishing priorities within the school's objectives;
● planning how objectives can be pursued within the school;
● organising the school and the staff so that efforts are co-ordinated towards securing objectives.

INTERPERSONAL SKILLS
These are necessary in order to ensure that staff morale and individual purpose and job satisfaction can be maintained through a period of enormous change in schools. Specifically, they can be brought to bear in:

● leading the staff through objective-setting and planning activities;
● motivating staff during the implementation of plans and programmes;
● acknowledging individual efforts and achievements.

Conceptual skills

(i) *The need to establish objectives*

The need to evolve a 'vision' of 'the school in future' stems from a number of sources. In addition to the requirements of strategic management, there is also the question of internal organisation and delegation. It is difficult to empower staff, to bring them into the decision-making processes and thereby use their knowledge, skills and experience in organisational problem-solving, if there is no clear agreement about objectives. It is important too that objectives unite, where possible, the concepts of effectiveness and efficiency outlined previously.

Hicks (1972) suggests that establishing managerial objectives for the organisation will resolve many of these difficulties:

> There will be many different ideas among members as to what the objectives of the organisation are or should be. Each person under such circumstances works towards his own idea of the organisational objectives. Much such work will be in conflicting directions or may be otherwise ineffective. Thus good objectives make behaviour in organisations more rational, more coordinated, and thus more effective, because everyone knows the accepted goals to work toward.

Drucker (1955) suggested that a business organisation faced with the problem of drawing up managerial objectives could approach it by accepting that though the detail must vary from one company to another, there were a number of areas in which objectives needed to be set. He outlined these as follows:

- market standing
- profitability
- productivity
- innovation
- physical and financial resource provision
- manager performance and development
- worker performance and attitudes
- public responsibility.

Holroyde (1976) has demonstrated that this approach could be adapted to work for a secondary school, though in a pre-local management context. Following financial devolution the relevance of this approach is probably increased. The table (Figure 2.2) indicates how the approach can be related to the process of drawing up objectives for a school.

Figure 2.2 Possible framework for establishing school objectives

Areas where specific objectives may prove useful

(1) Image and reputation (*Market standing*)
Relevant areas:
- with parents and pupils
- with employers and FE providers
- within the wider community
- with staff (teaching and non-teaching)
- with local industry and commerce*.

*Example** To develop links with local industry which bring industrialists into the school and provide opportunities for staff and pupils to gain first-hand experiences of industry.

(2) Effective use of resources (*Profitability*)
Relevant areas:
- identifying pupil needs
- evaluating the use made of pupils' time*
- identifying opportunities for action
- monitoring the response of the school to pupil needs.

*Example** To develop individualised learning programmes which reflect the needs and abilities of each pupil.

(3) Efficient use of resources (*Productivity*)
Relevant areas:
- use of staff time and abilities
- use of teaching approaches/technologies*
- use of space/facilities/equipment
- use of external resources within the school.

*Example** To deploy computers into teaching areas to encourage maximum use by teachers and pupils.

(4) Planned change (*Innovation*)
Relevant areas:
- curriculum development
- learning opportunities/teaching styles
- assessment, recording and reporting procedures*
- staffing structures
- systems and procedures.

*Example** To introduce a pupil self-assessment element into all courses in years 10 and 11 during the coming year.

(5) Resource provision (*Physical and financial resource provision*)
Relevant areas:
- budgetary planning
- fund-raising activities*
- income earning activities
- resource acquisition policy.

*Example** To collaborate with the parent–teacher association in organising one major fund-raising event each term.

(6) Staff development (*Manager performance and development*)
    Relevant areas:
      – staff development plan
      – individual development plans
      – training plans/courses*
      – job-related development
      – promotion and succession planning.
*Example** To produce a list of all LEA training opportunities for the coming year and to use this as a basis for discussing training priorities with each member of staff.

(7) Staff relations (*Worker performance and attitudes*)
    Relevant areas:
      – responsibilities and rewards
      – staff appraisal*
      – staff counselling
      – consultation procedures
      – communications.
*Example** To establish a system of staff appraisal which is consistent with national and local guidelines.

(8) Community relations (*Public responsibility*)
    Relevant areas:
      – within the school
      – within the neighbourhood
      – within the community*.
*Example** To develop a community action programme which provides appropriate help/assistance to groups within the community and fosters links between pupils and community members.

(ii) *How should objectives be evolved?*

It has already been noted that schools have traditionally nurtured a multiplicity of goals amongst staff, and securing agreement without appearing to be imposing external goals may be difficult. It is, however, important to try. Harrison (1978) lists the benefits of managerial objectives for the organisation, including such advantages as imbuing work with meaning and direction, and providing a basis for motivation; these are unlikely to arise if staff feel alienated by the way in which objectives are drawn up.

Terry (1972) underlines this point, concluding that, above all, objectives should be the result of participation by those who must carry them out, and should derive from and be supportive of the basic ethos of the organisation. The Education Reform Act 1988 would seem to place the power to approve or disapprove objectives with governors, but if the objectives are to be pursued with enthusiasm by teachers they will need to be evolved within the school.

There are of course many possible ways of securing teacher involvement in the process of objective setting. Which method is most appropriate will depend on the size of the school, its history, internal relationships and the qualities of staff at the different levels. What is important is that some method of obtaining consensus exists, that there is a shared commitment to the school's objectives. Harrison (*op. cit.*) suggests that there are a number of criteria which can be used to determine whether objectives have been well-conceived and properly formulated. These criteria can be applied to the school as follows:

Relevance   Do the objectives relate to and support the major purposes of the school?

Practicality   Do objectives realistically acknowledge the constraints?

Measurability Is there some way of counting progress towards the objectives?

Growth   Do the objectives provide for the development of the school rather than simply its continuance or survival?

Certainly, positive answers to these questions are more likely to be associated with positive attitudes by staff towards securing objectives.

But with devolution and the increased management functions of heads, there also comes a need for greater accountability at all levels within the school. What is clear here is that the school's objectives, once agreed, must become the basis for individual action and decision-making. A feature of the increased autonomy at school level is a corresponding loss of autonomy at teacher level. Teachers owe their best efforts towards securing the school's goals, whether they are personally in agreement with these goals or not.

What is important therefore, is to ensure that the method of agreeing objectives involves active participation by teachers, first to *legitimate* the objectives, and second to increase *commitment* amongst teachers towards securing these.

Legitimation can be increased by the process of objective-setting referred to above. Commitment will depend upon how the school is organised to pursue objectives, as well as what these objectives are. Steers and Porter (1983) suggest a number of actions which can help here: matching individual and organisation objectives, for example, by considering how individuals can be given opportunities to pursue those objectives which are personally meaningful to them. Underlining the links between personal and organisational objectives, and showing how individuals can develop their own careers through contributing to the organisation's development can also be helpful. It may be possible to 'compensate' some individuals for a loss of autonomy over objectives by a corresponding increase in freedom to determine how best to pursue these. This can help enhance the teacher's professionalism by focusing attention on pedagogy.

(iii) *How can objectives be changed/modified when necessary?*

Objectives, though less likely to change than the activities considered most appropriate to achieving them, nevertheless need to be kept under review. Unless the school's objectives continue to be regarded as relevant and realistic by teachers, it is likely that 'displacement' will occur – that is, individual teachers will substitute their own, more personal and tangible goals for what are seen as abstract organisational objectives. There is, therefore, a need to ensure that objectives are being altered in light of changing information or circumstances, and that any alterations have been clearly thought out, articulated and communicated to teachers. This in turn allows teachers to review their own roles and behaviours in light of the school's agreed purposes and objectives.

In particular, it is important to recognise that once objectives have been achieved they are no longer a useful guide to individual behaviour. In setting new objectives, therefore, the school needs to 'prune' away those which are no longer current; to ensure that the list of objectives does not become an expanding set of general statements about values and intent rather than a clear indication of current commitment.

Similarly, it may be that some objectives prove to be unattainable. It is quite possible that enthusiasm for a particular outcome will drive the school towards an objective which is simply too ambitious for its situation and resources. If objectives can be seen to be unattainable, then they need to be modified or revised to reflect what is actually possible. This does not mean removing a sense of challenge from the school's activities – objectives should be stretching and reflect the highest possible level of achievement – but it will not be helpful to maintain what are essentially 'pious hopes' within the school's pattern of objectives, as this is likely both to distort the direction of effort and to lower levels of morale and commitment.

Technical skills

(i) *Establishing priorities for action*

Though objectives will provide the start point for planning, the plans themselves can be formulated only if the school is able to take stock of its current position – it is necessary to know what are the current strengths and weaknesses of the school as well as where the school is going before decisions about priorities can be made. In this connection is may be helpful to distinguish between

- maintenance and development;
- the individual and the organisation;
- urgency and importance.

Though local management is an important new beginning for schools, it is not a blank sheet of paper. Requiring the school to produce, for example, a National Curriculum development plan does not relieve it of its obligation to ensure the continuity of many existing functions, objectives and activities. It will be necessary therefore to ensure that priorities reflect this balance between what needs to go on to *maintain* the school's current areas of effectiveness and efficiency, and what *development* can realistically be looked for beyond that. It would be unwise therefore, to place too much emphasis on new activities, if this leads to a neglect of existing areas of good practice, or if this encourages a level of expectations amongst staff which cannot be resourced from the school's budget. Establishing priorities therefore needs to be seen in the first instance as a preparation for the planning process, though subsequently it may become a part of this process.

There will also need to be attention to the differences and to the relationships between *individual* and *organisational objectives*. As previously stated, it is important in terms of motivation and commitment that individuals feel they are able to pursue individual goals. But it is equally important, in terms of organisational effectiveness, that organisational objectives are reflected in individual goals. The process of identifying priorities must marry these two dimensions. Argyris (1964) has suggested that this 'marriage' will be most fruitful where

- priorities are influenced by the organisation's past and future as well as the pressures of the immediate present;
- individuals have the capacity to influence both internally- and externally-orientated priorities;
- individuals are aware of the inter-relatedness of their differing priorities and the relationship of these priorities to overall objectives.

Finally, there is the need to be able to stand back from the enormous pressure for change and to ensure that the school is not simply reacting to outside influences. The school will need here to be able to distinguish between what is *urgent*, and what is fundamentally *important*. Of course, what is urgent must be addressed, but it must not be addressed at the expense of time and opportunity to consider those issues which will determine the long-term health and development of the school. The school's priorities must therefore include a medium- or longer-term emphasis which reflects the school's own values and beliefs, and not simply be a 'shopping list' of imperatives which have originated outside the school.

(ii) *Planning how objectives will be pursued*

Much has been written about planning as a managerial activity. It is important to note from the outset that planning is not forecasting. Though forecasting (predicting or projecting the future) is an important basis for planning, it is not in itself planning activity. The plan indicates not what the future is expected to be, but what *the organisation proposes to do in that expected future*. Thus to state that the school 'will be implementing the National Curriculum' does not constitute a curriculum plan – what is necessary is to know **what** it will be doing to implement, and **when**, and with **what resources**, and **through whom**. Fayol (1974) provided a definition of the planning function which draws these strands together:

> The plan of action is, at one and the same time, the result envisaged, the line of action to be followed, the stages to go through and the methods to use.

But is is not the definition of planning, but an understanding of how to set about it, which is of prime importance to school managers.

Harrison (*op. cit.*) outlines six 'dimensions' which, he argues, need to be understood and integrated within planning processes. These are time; level; subject; function; external environmental elements; and 'characteristics'. He goes on to outline what he means by 'characteristics' as follows.

Flexibility	Plans must be capable of reacting to changes in circumstances, information available and opportunity.
Cost effectiveness	Plans should cost less to prepare than the expected benefits of the planning process.
Rationality	Plans should relate in a clear and rational way to managerial objectives.

Comprehensiveness	A plan should cover all the relevant functions and levels within the organisation.
Specificity	A plan must state clearly what is to be done, when it is to be done, where it is to be done, how it is to be done, who is responsible for doing it.
Formality	A plan should be formally documented so that it can be seen by those responsible for its accomplishment.
Confidentiality	A plan should be available only to those who need to know about it.
Time span	A plan should include time constraints relating to the activities it includes.
Relevance	A plan should be clearly relevant to the perceived needs and priorities of the organisation.

These characteristics provide useful criteria against which the quality of a development plan could be assessed once it is compiled, but little indication about how to compile it. There are models which can be helpful here, however. Drucker (1955), for example, has suggested a way of approaching decision-making which can be readily adapted to the planning function.

Decision-making, he suggests, involves a number of stages or processes, namely:

(1) Define the problem. Analyse it into symptoms and causes, and locate the 'critical factor'.
(2) Determine the conditions for its solution, the need to meet objectives and the balance between present and future.
(3) Analyse the problem; find the facts necessary to a solution and capable of being obtained. Know where the facts stop and assumptions begin.
(4) Develop alternative solutions, as many as possible, including 'do nothing'.
(5) Choose between solutions using as criteria for choice: risk, economy of effort, timing, and limitation of resources.
(6) Make the solution effective.

These stages can be used to develop a conceptual map of the stages involved in planning (see Figure 2.3).

Two important points emerge from looking at planning in this way. First it can be seen that in each of the six stages identified there is not merely scope for participation by those who will be affected by the plan,

Figure 2.3 Stages in the planning process

Decision making	Key question	Planning process
1. Define the problem, identify its causes and symptoms	Where are we now?	Establish the current situation
2. Determine conditions for a satisfactory solution	Where do we need to go from here?	Review agreed objectives and priorities
3. Analyse the problem, gather together information needed for its solution	What do we need to know before we proceed?	Analyse the current situation in light of agreed objectives and priorities
4. Develop alternative solutions (as many as possible)	What options are available?	Identify the possible alternative actions available

5. Choose between solutions, using agreed criteria	Which is the best option?	1. Evaluate alternatives in light of
		  (i) expected contribution to objectives
		  (ii) costs of implementation
		2. Select 'best' alternative

6. Make the solution 'effective'	How can we realise the best option?	Implement selected alternative

but that the *quality* of planning is likely to significantly improve if there is active participation. Thus a better picture of the present situation is likely to be obtained if all those able to provide a perspective are consulted; the range and quality of options put forward for consideration are also likely to be enhanced if there is direct involvement by different groups and individuals. Indeed, given the increasingly diverse nature of educational activities it is questionable whether any meaningful evaluation of the alternatives is possible without 'expert' advice from teachers, whose specialised knowledge and experience will be a vital source of information to senior managers.

The second point, however, concerns the nature of managerial accountability and its place within a participative process. Stage 5.2, selecting the 'best' alternative, is where the head, or perhaps the senior management team, needs to accept responsibility for deciding the most appropriate course of action. It may well be that some of those who have participated in the previous stages, for example by developing alternatives, will be disappointed by the decision taken. It is important therefore to communicate to staff *before* the planning process begins that participation in the process will not mean acquiring a vote – meaningful participation is aimed at improving overall effectiveness, not following what the majority or a group of teachers would prefer. In turn, however, it will be important for those responsible for drawing up the school's development plan to be aware that successful implementation is more likely if staff feel that there has been meaningful participation in the planning process. They should also remember that in selecting alternatives they become accountable to the staff for the consequences of decisions made, and should be prepared to accept the responsibility should things go wrong as readily as the credit should things go well.

(iii) *Developing appropriate structures and roles*

In addition to objective-setting and planning skills, the manager of the self-determining school will need to be able to create an organisation which encourages staff to pursue school priorities and which supports them in this process. This could well mean that 'traditional' school structures will be replaced during the next few years by a more diverse and calculated range of alternative approaches to school organisation. Insofar as traditional structures seem, above all, to reflect salary structures rather than to be thought-out responses to the school's own priorities, some will feel that such a review is long overdue. Of course there will still be, in the short term at least, pressures to reflect previous numbers and levels of staff within any new pattern of deployment, so the transition may take some time.

However, the need to promote effectiveness at all levels requires a structure which has been designed to do just this – not one which compromises between a senior group whose jobs are defined in relation to the school's purposes and the teachers whose jobs are defined in terms of activities. The organisation of the school around major school objectives, and the definition of all roles within the structure in terms of their relationships to these objectives, is a pre-requisite for managing individual effort, and must be tackled.

Again, Drucker (*op. cit.*) provides a useful start point. Given that the manager understands the objectives to be pursued, three questions need to be asked.

(1) What activities will be required to achieve the purposes of the organisation?
(2) What decisions about these activities will need to be made?
(3) What relationships need to be created/maintained between the people carrying out these activities?

Drucker goes on to suggest that addressing these questions implies either 'federal' or 'functional' decentralisation – that is, organising around objectives, or around functions which contribute to a number of objectives. In both cases, Drucker's advice is simple: ensure that each member of the organisation knows what his/her responsibilities are and how these relate to the organisation's purposes; ensure that decisions are located as far down in the structure as is feasible; ensure that individuals understand the contributions to and from the work of others which will be required.

Roles within the structure, then, are defined in terms of purposes, either directly or indirectly, and are backed up with the authority necessary to make those decisions likely to arise. The organisation thus provides each member of staff with an area for action (accountability) and a basis for action (authority). It does not necessarily provide an 'approved method' for doing the job – individuals are (within limits) free to determine 'means' for themselves, so long as they are securing the agreed purposes.

Is is possible, then, for any two schools of similar size, with similar purposes, to adopt quite different methods of organising. What matters is that in any one school the method adopted provides a vehicle for achieving organisational purposes and can be operated by the staff available. Healthy organisation is therefore a function of what *the organisation makes possible*, not conforming to a particular pattern which replicates the average preference of all schools. Determining whether the current organisational structure is healthy or not can be approached by considering the extent to which the school's structure reflects certain principles. Carlson (1967) has identified a number of such principles, which he calls tests of organisational effectiveness. These include:

ACCOUNTABILITY Is each department organised around the achievement of a major company objective for which a single executive is held finally responsible and accountable in conformity with definite standards?

AUTHORITY Is there a clear line of formal authority running from the top to the bottom of the organisation? Does everyone know exactly to whom he/she reports, what he is accountable for, and what standards he/she is required to meet?

PROGRESSION Do all positions within each department, and the company as a whole, provide a natural ladder of progression and increasing scope so related in sequence of difficulty that at all times employees are in training for advancements as vacancies occur?

RELATIONSHIPS Have all functional responsibilities, relationships, and authorities been clarified? Are lines of command, sources of advice, and channels of communication definite and clear-cut?

EFFECTIVENESS Does the Organisation Structure (pattern) create a climate that encourages maximum executive performance, effectiveness and accountability?

Though these principles may seem somewhat foreign to current school structures, it is clear that self-management brings with it a need to see 'organising' as the first and possibly most important managerial task to be tackled. It will be vital to the school's prospects that its management team understand this responsibility, and are able to respond to it creatively and confidently. Subjecting the school's structure to Carlson's tests may be a good place to start.

Interpersonal skills

Given that teaching staff account for about 80 per cent of school spending, it is clear that getting the best out of those staff is a major determinant of the school's effectiveness. Though the contribution by teachers will be greater where the school has agreed purposes and established appropriate plans, there is still an important role to be played by the quality of personal relationships. Indeed, many studies suggest that the quality of commitment from staff, and hence performance from staff, is essentially a product of attitudes and relationships, rather than resources (see for example Likert, 1967; Hersey and Blanchard, 1972).

It is nevertheless still true that the majority of senior staff in schools have little formal training in personal and interpersonal skills. Nor, if Ann Jones's survey is representative (Jones, 1987), do head-teachers see this as the main training priority – understanding new technologies and evaluation skills were the most highly ranked needs amongst her sample group (to which living with LMS can probably be added today). Yet the same heads were unanimous in identifying 'motivating staff', 'resolving conflict' and 'negotiating' as the three most important skills of headship. We have here then a slightly curious position: head-teachers, it seems, recognise the importance of interpersonal competence, but either feel they were born with this, or have acquired it via osmosis, since there are few who have undertaken training in this area or taken other direct action to develop/acquire the relevant skills. More curious still, many of these head-teachers are more comfortable in the role of 'leading professional' – a position which would require a very high level of personal relationships with staff – than of 'school manager', a role one can conceivably fulfil satisfactorily through sheer technical competence. It is important therefore to consider some of the major areas of interpersonal competence, and to underline the need for senior staff in school to develop skills in these areas, both because this will improve the level and quality of pupil experience and the level of satisfaction teachers experience from their work.

Finding appropriate organising categories for these skills is difficult – many interpersonal skills seem to be equally relevant across a range of contexts and of situations. There is, therefore, inevitable overlap however the issue is approached, but the functions of leadership, motivating staff and providing feedback to staff seem sufficiently important to merit separation, whatever the problems.

(i) *Leading the staff group*

Leadership is most often defined as the process of influencing group behaviour towards a common goal. It is worthwhile to distinguish here between leadership and management – there is no necessity that the goal be appropriate or even sensible, since leadership is independent of the quality of goal. (The 'Charge of the Light Brigade' is an instructive example of the difference – a splendid example of leadership but, on reflection, possibly not the best management.) Leadership is then a skill which managers will find extremely useful, though it will not in itself compensate for a lack of managerial judgement.

There is a considerable body of literature concerning leadership available, though most is based on research studies carried out in the United States; Stodgill (1974) and Yukl (1981) offer the most detailed summaries; Hersey and Blanchard (1972), Blake and Mouton (1964) and Fiedler (1967) put forward the most convincing theories. In the United Kingdom, Adair (1983) has produced a useful framework for thinking about the leader's role and relationships, and his Functional Leadership Model has been widely drawn on in training situations.

Contemporary approaches to leadership, whilst not rejecting the natural advantages which can be available to those with appropriate physical attributes or personality features (the so-called personality or trait approach), identify three major variables:

- the leader's attitudes towards the task;
- his/her relationship with the work group; and
- the context or situation.

Leader effectiveness is determined by the way these three variables fit together or interact with one another – it is a product of the leader's ability to alter his/her approach according to the needs of the situation and the characteristics of the work group. This means, of course, that there is no one best leadership style – so training for leadership must be about developing a range of different behaviours and skills rather than learning 'how to do it'.

This research would seem to be relevant for senior staff in schools on three counts. First, because it suggests that to a significant degree leadership qualities can be developed. Training therefore is both vital and worthwhile, and should perhaps be a requirement. Second, because it seems to indicate that a variety of different approaches to leadership will be necessary if leader effectiveness is to be maintained. Head-teachers who treat each challenge or issue alike are unlikely to bring the best out of the staff group. Third, though it is necessary to have a range of leadership approaches to select from, the way in which the selection is made should be based on a systematic analysis of the situation and so therefore the differences in approach should conform to a pattern. It is the recognition of this pattern by staff which should truly be regarded as consistency. Simply behaving in the same way irrespective of circumstances should more properly be called inflexibility.

Further, two specific points emerging from leadership theory would seem to have direct relevance for head-teachers in the present climate. The first, deriving from the work of Hersey and Blanchard (1972), relates to the notion of 'maturity'. Hersey and Blanchard's research suggested that the leadership approach which most often produced good results with 'immature' staff was strongly directive and task orientated. This is important because in a very real sense the changes which are taking place in schools are rendering staff of all ages and experience levels newly 'immature'. This may then be a time when firm direction 'from the top' will be needed in order to prompt staff into the necessary planning activities, and very clear guidance on goals will be necessary to secure high levels of commitment. Conversely this would seem to be an inappropriate time to invite staff generally to consider how the school should respond to the multiple demands of curriculum, assessment and managerial changes, as disagreement, fragmentation and, in some cases, despair might ensue.

The second point relates to the 'tradition' in schools of setting up working parties or consultative groups to consider a wide range of issues. Much of the research into leadership suggests that there are issues which are simply not amenable to group decision-making. Either the decision should be 'announced' by the leader or delegated to the person with the most appropriate knowledge, experience and interest. Trying to get a work group to feel 'involved' or to participate can be counter-productive in such circumstances. The demands that a consensus-seeking approach to decision-making place on individuals should not be under-estimated. Often staff, feeling pressured into taking an active interest in the issue and also constrained to maintain friendly relationships with other group members, would prefer to be told what to do, or left to get on with it, so long as it does not mean yet another meeting.

(ii) *Motivating staff*

Clearly, the quality and style of leadership experienced by staff will be one major factor in determining motivational levels. But, as mentioned above, leadership, though an important management tool, will not necessarily suffice. Positive action must be taken to create a climate in which teachers feel both committed to and confident about the school's objectives, and ready to implement the programmes which follow from these.

A number of perspectives on what contributes to the motivational levels of staff have been developed and, in recent years, there have been attempts to assess the relevance of these perspectives for the motivation of teachers. Dean (1985) reviews the most frequently quoted theories of motivation and puts forward a list of possible motivators, though she suggests that some of the more important factors will often be beyond the influence of the school. Everard and Morris (1985) produce a somewhat fuller account of the approaches of Maslow (1954), McGregor (1960), Herzberg (1966) and McClelland (1961) and offer advice to school managers based on these:

> We should remember to use the 'motivators' – i.e. people's need for achievement, recognition, responsibility, job interest, personal growth and advancement potential. We tend to underestimate the needs of other people in these areas. Involving others in decisions which affect them is one way of meeting all or most of these needs.

Jones (1987) pointed out that the head-teachers in her survey identified motivating staff as the most important skill needed within the job (though, as mentioned previously, this was not seen as the main priority area for training), and Torrington and Weightman (1989) suggest that

> Most schools are suffering from innovation overload, at the same time as their staffs' morale is generally at lower ebb than it has been for a long time.

What would seem to be needed, then, are specific ideas about what school managers might do to create a climate within the school conducive to high levels of commitment from staff and then to trigger staff into such commitment. Inevitably, however, these questions will require different answers in different school settings, perhaps even between different teachers in the same school setting. No one approach, nor one theory of motivation is likely to prove enduringly effective with all staff, even in the smaller school. What would seem important therefore is that senior staff in schools are aware of the many approaches which have been successful, and the circumstances in which these successes have been recorded. The notion of teachers as largely self-motivating professionals needs to be set aside, and information about and training focused on how to get the best out of staff should be much more widely available to school managers. This means accepting that individual performance levels are crucially influenced by attitudes and school climate as well as the skills and resources available. It is also necessary to recognise that, as motivation is associated with high levels of job satisfaction, the quality of the teachers' working experiences as well as the quality of the school's outputs may hinge upon the senior staff's skills in this area.

Steers and Porter (1983), following a wide-ranging survey of motivation theory, offer a number of conclusions which can help senior staff in schools to decide whether their current approach is likely to be successful. Three of these seem particularly apposite to the challenge of motivating teachers. First, is there a commitment to 'manage' motivational processes – an acceptance that there needs to be a conscious and deliberate strategy in this area? The commitment level of staff is thus seen as an *outcome* of successful management performance, not an input to it. Second, is sufficient attention paid to *individual differences*? The relevance of 'rewards' needs to be considered in relation to the individual teacher's needs, abilities, personal characteristics and situation. Third, are teachers invited to take on tasks which offer appropriate challenges? High performance levels are most often associated with the achievement of important *personal satisfactions* via work experiences.

(iii) *Acknowledging individual achievements*

There is, then, a weight of evidence from studies of motivational patterns that individual commitment and satisfaction will be encouraged by some system for identifying individual goals and for giving feedback to the individual on progress towards these goals. Though this could be achieved in a variety of ways, clearly current developments towards teacher appraisal have enormous potential to offer.

Generalising from the recent pilot studies in six local education authorities, the National Steering Group for Teacher Appraisal (1989) listed as key benefits:

> ... greater confidence and improved morale for teachers

and

> ... better professional relations and communication within the school.

The evaluation of the pilot schemes identified many teachers who reported positive responses to the appraisal process. Such respondents typically stated that appraisal had made them more self-aware and lent a sharper and more critical focus to their thinking and planning. Many of these teachers went on to say that this, in turn, had made them more aware of the needs of others and of the school as a whole. The appraisal process had thus served to give teachers a clearer view of their job, their aims and what was expected of them, and of the aims of the school. Some teachers see this increased awareness as the first step towards accepting and initiating changes in practice.

Another frequently mentioned psychological effect of appraisal was a resulting 'boost' to morale.

Our interviewees have spoken of improved self-esteem, increased confidence, reassurance, a sense of support, praise and recognition as aspects of improved morale resulting from appraisal. (Bradley *et al.*, 1989)

Managed properly then, the introduction of teacher appraisal into the school can provide exciting opportunities for teachers and school managers alike. As well as providing scope for specific, meaningful feedback to teachers, it can have important motivational benefits and, through increasing the amount and quality of dialogue between staff about goals, roles and achievements, improve communications within the school. Further, it can provide an important vehicle for channelling teacher effort towards school priorities – whether these relate to the development planning process itself or to activities which derive from this process. Some practical suggestions on how appraisal can be introduced and integrated into school life can be found in West and Bollington (1990).

Summary

In responding to the changes that are occurring in education we have argued that the school will need to be reconceptualised as a management structure and that correspondingly head-teachers need to see their roles as being managerial in nature. Drawing on developments from non-educational sources we have also suggested some of the management skills that will be necessary in the new context. These are seen as being concerned with conceptual, technical and interpersonal competencies, and will need to be blended with educational knowledge and experience to forge a new perspective on educational management.

CHAPTER THREE

Educational Management: The Evolving Role

So far we have argued that recent legislation has fundamentally altered the relationship between schools and their local education authorities, and that a particularly important feature of this altered relationship is the need to 'manage' educational provision at school level. This has immediate significance for the roles of head-teachers and other senior staff in schools, who will need to develop the skills needed to protect and to promote the school in an educational 'marketplace'.

It has also been argued that many of these skills are management skills, and that schools can therefore profitably consider management practices and models which have evolved in organisations where market conditions have always obtained. There are many opportunities to draw on practices developed in other environments, and these can be useful in helping school managers to develop approaches to conceptualising the school's goals, organising to achieve these goals, and involving staff creatively and meaningfully in these processes.

Nevertheless, it is important to remember that techniques and approaches borrowed from elsewhere are essentially tools – means rather than ends. Indeed there are those who have questioned the extent to which 'conventional management practice' has any relevance for the regulation of educational establishments. Taylor (1976) was one of the first to suggest caution:

> Plainly there is much to be gained from the greater awareness and self-consciousness of social process to which managerial analysis and prescriptions give rise. But precisely because such approaches offer the possibility of order and enhanced control in situations that are often anxiety-creating, problematic and ambiguous, they are likely to be taken up and applied with somewhat uncritical enthusiasm, with possibly unforeseen and illiberal consequences that are inimical to values embodied in the broader educative task of the school.

More recently (and with a deal less caution) Bottery (1988) has taken up this theme:

> Within current approaches to management in the schools is a dangerously explosive mixture with which only those who are not concerned about the education of the majority of the population's children, or of the job satisfaction and professional development of their teachers, can be happy.

To a degree such criticisms have been overtaken by the fundamental changes in responsibilities and power relationship which have taken place – head-teachers are *de facto* 'managers' of their schools under recent legislation, whether or not this is considered appropriate by all members of the educational community. There is, nevertheless, a need to ensure that management thinking and approaches culled from other environments best serve rather than lead those who exercise stewardship over schools. Thus, the challenge is to learn how to exercise managerial authority in order to nurture and to develop what is valued in education, rather than to 'control' and 'direct' teacher effort towards a narrowly defined and predominantly efficiency-led series of goals. But it is vital that we do not confuse 'narrowness' with the need to focus effort. The fact that a school chooses to organise itself around the pursuit of a small number of appropriate, high quality goals is not evidence of such narrowness, but a reflection of its understanding of the need to establish priorities and to maintain, from one planning period to another, continuity between priorities so that real achievement is possible.

Priorities in schools

The start point for management then, must be a series of priorities for the school. As previously argued, how these priorities are arrived at within the school is itself a crucial issue. Bush (1986), pointing out that establishing purposes for educational institutions has therefore been a major strand in the development of an educational management literature, notes that

> There is disagreement, though, about the value of *formal* statements of purpose, about *whose* purposes may become the objectives of the organisation and about how the institution's goals are determined.

Such 'disagreement' can probably be minimised if these issues are tackled in reverse order – decisions about how goals are to be determined need to come first (and to be acceptable to staff), so that the 'formal' statements are an outcome of the goal-setting process rather than abstract statements of intent, however admirable the intention. The School Development Planning Project report (Hargreaves *et al.*, 1989) suggests that development planning offers one way of working through this process:

> The distinctive feature of a development plan (DP) is that it brings together *in an overall plan*, national and LEA policies and initiatives, the school's aims and values, its existing achievements and its needs for development. By coordinating aspects of planning which are otherwise quite separate, the school acquires a shared sense of direction and is able to control and manage the tasks of development and change. Priorities for development are planned in detail for one year and are supported by action plans or working documents for staff. The priorities for later years are sketched to outline the longer term programme.

Though the emphasis here on 'control' may be disquieting to those who favour a more 'spontaneous' basis for teacher action, we need to accept that 'control' is not necessarily antithetical to the notion of teachers using their own creativity, experience and professional judgement within the context of agreed whole-school priorities. Indeed it can be argued that a feature of school structures to date has been the degree to which a failure to understand management principles has inhibited opportunities for real involvement in decision-making. In the absence of a clear definition of purposes, head-teachers have been seen as unwilling, or perhaps unable, to delegate. This is hardly surprising, as it is difficult to trust staff with decisions where there has been little discussion of what the school is trying to achieve. In such circumstances, 'control' tends to be externally applied and seeks to regulate or guide behaviours. Apart from the inherent inefficiency of this approach (since it requires time and energy to 'police' behaviour), it is one which is likely to cause staff considerable frustration. This is a vital area of concern for the self-managing school.

The empowerment of staff

Creating a structure which tackles this problem will need a commitment towards empowering staff – that is, defining areas of accountability and practising real delegation.

We can observe from management practice in other environments how important delegation is in securing an effective and efficient decision structure (which also, via involvement in that decision structure, can increase levels of commitment and motivation). But delegation is most likely to be practised where there is a high quality of goal definition, since it is easier to trust staff to make appropriate decisions where there is agreement about what is to be achieved. In chapter two, it was suggested that it is difficult to 'empower' in this way unless staff shared a common understanding of the school's goals. It is vital therefore that the management of the school is seen as a process to which many members of staff contribute through their own decision-making. In this way it can be ensured that management is not restrictive, limiting the autonomy of individuals within the school system. Rather it is developmental, encouraging members of staff to use their own professional skills and experience to make decisions which are informed by and consistent with whole-school policies. This can significantly enrich the quality of the individual teacher's work experience, as well as providing a more reliable management development vehicle than the piece-meal course attendance, unrelated to the day-to-day concerns of the job, which for so many teachers is called management development. It will also, as has been previously argued, help to create a climate in which staff become committed to achieving organisational goals.

These benefits will only accrue if the school understands and practises real delegation. Staff must therefore be encouraged to pass on and to accept authority, whilst recognising that is it not possible to 'shed' accountability for decisions taken on their behalf by subordinates. The start point for delegation must be, then, a clear agreement about the outcomes which are required, as without this there is no basis for trust (from the superior) or for decision-making (for the subordinate). Of course, delegation involves more than this (it is advisable, for example, to agree what resources will be available, how outcomes will be measured, time-scales for review etc, and to inform others who may be affected). It is however impossible to establish a decision-making structure unless senior management are willing to make the authority to decide and to act, albeit in specific circumstances and with specific goals, widely available throughout the school organisation.

A model for educational management

The distinctive feature of educational management is, then, the process through which appropriate goals are identified – in simple terms, establishing what is meant by 'effectiveness' for the particular school. This is by no means a straightforward process. Currently, though guided by national and local requirements, school governors and head-teachers are accountable for identifying what these goals should be; and is, for deciding locally what constitutes effectiveness for that particular school.

Figure 3.1   A model for educational management

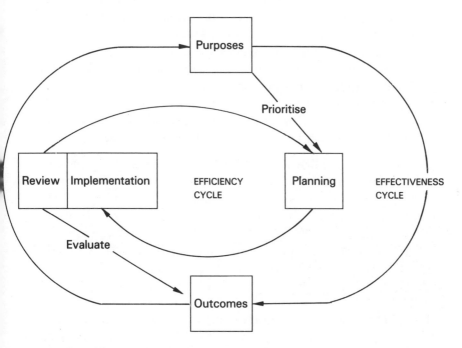

Purposes Educational goals, locally determined, but reflecting national requirements
Planning Selecting priorities within these goals and translating these into programmes for action
Implementation Allocating resources and deploying staff within the programmes
Review Monitoring that resources and staff are being used to maximum advantage within the programmes
(Implementation and Review processes are likely to interact constantly with, and thereby influence, each other)
Outcomes The impact of the school's activities on the educational goals selected

Within the framework of these goals, which though they may be similar may nevertheless differ significantly between schools, there will be a series of common managerial challenges. These challenges relate to how the school can be most efficiently managed in pursuit of the agreed goals. It is possible to represent these two components, and the relationship between them as shown in Figure 3.1.

Overall management performance will be determined by three sets of relationships:

(1)   The extent to which the school's *purposes* reflect educational needs, requirements and opportunities, and the degree to which the

outcomes secured in pursuit of these purposes (at least some of which are likely to be unplanned) appear to match intentions. A crucial element will be the quality of judgement school managers are able to bring to bear on these processes.

(2) The extent to which the school's use of resources constitutes an *efficient process-model*. A much more sophisticated analysis of input–output relationships will be needed here.

(3) The overlaps between *plans and purposes* and the *implementation of plans and the desired outcomes*. Crucial elements here will be establishing priorities and evaluating outcomes in light of purposes.

There is, then, an efficiency cycle, which is amenable to conventional management approaches and analysis; and an effectiveness cycle, which is more problematic, relies heavily on values, and the 'success' of which is likely to be measurable (if at all) only over extended periods of time.

Yet the school can thrive only if efficient resource use is seen as a mediating variable and both processes and outcomes are monitored. Two sorts of 'measure' of management effectiveness are therefore desirable, and simplistic judgements about school performance are likely to be unreliable.

It is likely, however, that judgements about the school's effectiveness will be made by a number of groups – the LEA, governors, parents, the wider community – though it is equally likely that these groups will have different amounts and qualities of information available and will apply different criteria. Performance Indicators seem certain to be used in this context, but this will not necessarily simplify the problem, since the indicators of educational output cannot be viewed as precise or finite in the way that, say, the range of subjects available (an input) within a curriculum can. It is, after all, one thing to suspect that social factors influence the performance levels of schools, quite another to estimate in which directions, and by how much.

Jesson and Mayston (1990) offer sensible advice, arguing that 'a coherent set of performance indicators' will only be possible if three conditions are satisfied. These are:

(i) A clear conceptual framework within which the indicators are derived.
(ii) A selection process to determine which indicators are to be applied and how.
(iii) A specification of how the indicators fit into the management and decision process.

Jesson and Mayston (1990)

It may however be more realistic to accept that no such coherent set exists. Rather, each school (in consultation with governors, parents and other interest groups) will need to develop its own understanding of the component parts of the educational management model.

A key factor will be the recognition, in developing this understanding, that effective management, though drawing on skills and techniques, is in the end to do with ways of thinking about the school, and of linking thought to action. Cave and Wilkinson (1990) suggest that

> ... what the headteacher needs is not training in specific techniques but a broad understanding of the concepts, language and principles required to monitor and control the activities necessary to carry out the new functions and to evaluate the outcomes.

Our own view is that head-teachers will need all this *and* training in specific techniques, since neither the understanding without the skills to operate the model nor the operational skills without any understanding of the wider purposes of the school constitute a satisfactory basis for educational management. Nor is this broadening of the head-teacher role, and its accompanying drive for a definition (or redefinition) which goes beyond that of 'curriculum leader' restricted to Britain. In Canada, Holmes and Wynne (1989) describe the need for a similar marriage of educational vision and managerial competence, observing that

> ... if the school administration stands for nothing the school will inevitably be overtaken by those with sufficient power who do stand for something ... It is already becoming evident that retreat to value-neutrality will not assure the common school's future; the retreat from values in urban, public schools leads to increased enrolment in special schools (both public and private) with a clear sense of direction.

Caldwell and Spinks (1988), reflecting on the Effective Resource Allocation in Schools Project (ERASP) carried out in Australia, provide a further echo of this theme:

> Many well-intentioned goal-setting and policy-making endeavours in the past have resulted in disappointment, if not cynicism, as the results gather dust because of the absence of an approach to school management which ensures that plans and budgets reflect goals and policies.

We detect in these comments the same trend towards greater autonomy for head-teachers accompanied by a sharper and more direct accountability for their decisions that has become a major feature of post-ERA school development in Britain. The challenge is to evolve educational management not separately from, but in harmony with this trend. This is underlined in the Report of the School Management Task Force (Styan *et al.*, 1990):

> ... there is a case for development activities specifically targeted at the needs of heads, but they must not lead to the creation of a separate managerial cadre, distancing heads from the school staff. School management requires a team approach, with the head reliant on the specialist expertise of colleagues.

Much hangs on the way head-teachers and other senior staff in schools respond to this challenge. Locally, it may be the difference between a particular school growing and developing or simply fading away. Nationally it has enormous significance for the quality of educational experience which will be offered to a generation of young people now in our schools. There would seem to be scope for significant 'borrowings' from management practice developed in other environments which can help, but approaches and techniques brought in from elsewhere will need to be applied carefully and sensitively, and in a secure educational framework. Building security at school and national levels will centre on our ability to develop appropriate educational goals and to communicate these to all those involved in the educational enterprise. Management is the vehicle which will allow us to achieve these goals.

Summary

This chapter has addressed some of the anxieties about 'managerialism' which have been expressed. It has suggested that management approaches can be used to advance, rather than subjugate, educational policies, by paying proper attention to the processes through which priorities are set for the school and for individuals, and creating an 'empowered' staff group. Further, it suggests that a major responsibility of management is to provoke educational debate.

It puts forward a model outlining the relationship between educational goals and outcomes and management activities, and will draw upon this model in subsequent chapters as the key managerial processes of planning, implementing and reviewing are explored in more detail.

PART TWO

Managing School Development: Methods and Approaches

So far we have considered the changes that are influencing the work of schools and examined the implications for those who have management roles. This has led us to pinpoint an apparent contradiction with, on the one hand, schools being required to work within more centrally prescribed curriculum policies, whilst, on the other, having much greater control over their own resources. Though this trend can create tensions, it also provides opportunities and challenges that may well facilitate improvements in schooling.

Our concern, therefore, is with finding positive ways of responding to these new opportunities, ways that can help schools to meet the challenges that arise. With this aim in mind we have examined evidence from non-educational settings that may provide some useful leads. In outlining these ideas, however, we have stressed the need to keep in mind the unique tasks faced by schools and teachers.

At the core of any such developments are likely to be matters related to the curriculum. In this context we use the term 'curriculum' rather generally to refer to all the planned learning opportunities provided for pupils. School developments are also likely to be concerned with the use of resources, in particular human resources, in order to facilitate improvements in the curriculum that is offered.

Bearing all of this in mind, our proposals are based upon a model of *educational* management that seeks to set approaches for improving efficiency within a context that continually reminds us of the wider purposes of schooling. It is vital therefore that each school debates these issues, and that the parameters to be used to delineate *effectiveness* – how purposes are to be defined and what criteria can be applied to assess

43

outcomes – are continually discussed and refined at school level. This process could be described as ensuring that appropriate *management thinking* pervades the school, and it also provides the context for *management action*. In the following chapters therefore we will focus on management in action, the three interrelated processes which make up what we have called the 'efficiency cycle' – review, planning and implementation. In particular we will be examining ways in which these three processes can be managed in order to bring about developments in school policies and practice.

CHAPTER FOUR

Beginning the Cycle: The Review Stage

In the previous chapter we suggested that efficient use of the school's resources could be promoted through a cycle of planning, implementing and reviewing school policies. In an ideal world, the newly established school would be able to identify its purposes and then move into planning to start this cycle. However, schools are already functioning, and it is not possible to erase what has gone before and to start with a blank sheet of paper.

The first priority therefore is to break into the cycle (see Figure 4.1). We have chosen to do this at the review stage for two reasons. First, because review can be seen as coming at both the beginning and the end of the planning process, which, though we break it up for study purposes, is in fact a continuous and seamless circle of activity. Second, because it seems reasonable to start by asking 'what happens at present?' We start with the review therefore as the stage where we gather information that can

Figure 4.1   The efficiency cycle

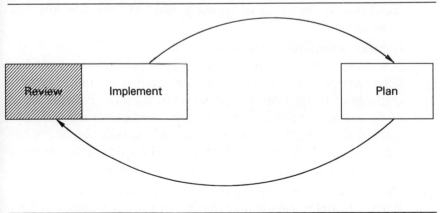

inform the processes of planning and implementing plans for development.

It is important to note, at this point, that whilst the need to address a particular concern at a given time may lead to a deliberate strategy for gathering information, often much of the information that is needed will already be available in other forms or for other purposes. It is because of this wealth of information generated by the school's activities that the process of review can be a seen as a continuing feature of the life of a school. Central to the task of management should be to create procedures that encourage the monitoring of existing policies in order to evaluate their effectiveness.

Choosing review methods

How, then, should the school approach such investigations? There is a wide range of possible review methods and the aim must be to choose one which is appropriate to the purposes at hand. This choice is likely to be influenced by the following factors:

(1) **The nature of the topic that is under review**

Some topics will be relatively straight-forward, thus lending themselves to be examined by methods that involve simply the gathering of factual information. So, for example, a review of how frequently the school library is used at particular times in the week may be undertaken by recording use on some form of tally sheet. However, many aspects of school life require much more complex and sensitive methods if they are to be reviewed. Often matters of policy will be perceived in different ways by different members of the school community. Consequently understanding these policies requires us to find ways of taking account of these multiple perspectives.

(2) **Contextual features of the school**

Schools vary from one another in many ways. Apart from obvious differences of size, shape and location, there is an individuality in each school arising from its traditions and the collective experiences of its staff and pupils. In choosing an appropriate method for a particular review, therefore, it is necessary to take account of this individuality. A method that will be ideal for one school organisation may cause very negative reactions in another

(3) **The level of previous knowledge and experience available**

When a school is seeking to review an area of policy about which it already has considerable experience it is likely that the emphasis will be on collecting and making sense of knowledge that is already present. Procedures for drawing together information can be based on structures and category systems drawn from this experience and knowledge. If, on the other hand, the matters to be reviewed are relatively new to the school, a more open-ended perspective may be appropriate. This means that those involved in the review may have to collect general information without having a clear focus to their investigations.

(4) **The management style adopted in the school**

If it is to be conducted in a way that will facilitate further action, it is important that the review process is carried out in ways that will be comfortable for those involved. Consequently it is important to adopt approaches that are consistent with the school's usual ways of doing things. A review process that necessitates high levels of participation in a school that is normally characterised by a directive management style, for example, is likely to run into difficulty.

Keeping these four factors in mind, methods for review should be chosen that:

- relate to the questions that need to be answered;
- are feasible in the time that is available;
- will be acceptable to those who are likely to be involved;
- are not too disruptive to the day-to-day life of the school.

It also makes sense to review the methods themselves, in order to be aware of their strengths and weaknesses. Common sense would suggest that whatever approach is used will have its limitations. To be aware of such limitations is a start point for assessing the value of the information that is collected.

In this section we provide an introduction to methods that might be used to gather information as part of a review process. We must stress, however, that our aim is *not* to provide prescriptions but rather to suggest some ways in which appropriate approaches can be developed within schools.

As we have indicated there is a range of approaches that can be used as part of the review process. The following eight approaches seem to us to be the most useful:

- using published review schedules
- using an audit matrix
- holding meetings

- using questionnaires
- interviewing staff
- observing classrooms
- analysing documents
- using 'outsiders'.

We will now comment on each of these methods. Figure 4.2 provides a summary of their advantages and limitations, plus some sources of advice and examples.

(i) *Using published review schedules*

One way of collecting together and collating information that already exists within a school regarding an aspect of policy and/or practice is to use some form of schedule. One of the most widely used sources of such schedules in the GRIDS project (i.e. Guidelines for Review and Internal Development in Schools) (McMahon *et al.*, 1984; Abbott *et al.*, 1989). This project developed materials and procedures that can be used to help teachers to review the curriculum and school organisation. Central to this approach is a recommendation that staff should not attempt to make a detailed review of all aspects of a school at once. Instead they are advised to identify one or two areas that they consider to be priorities for specific review and development, tackle these first, evaluate what they have achieved, and then select another priority. The main information-gathering instruments used are typically survey sheets completed by the whole staff during the initial review stage. Whilst we accept that schedules of this sort may be useful, we feel that there are occasions when it would be more beneficial for staff within a school to develop their own, adopting formats and headings that are directly relevant to the situation within the particular school.

(ii) *Using an audit matrix*

In recent years there has been increasing attention on accountability issues in education. There is, therefore, often a need for the school to be able to reassure itself that, for example, pupils are receiving a balanced curriculum or that cross-curricular themes or dimensions are being made available to all pupils. A particularly useful approach to this form of review is the composition of a matrix on which pupil experiences can be 'mapped'. In this way a picture of one aspect of the school's functioning can be developed. Many aspects of the school's life are amenable to

Figure 4.2 School review – selecting an appropriate method

Method	Advantage	Limitations	Sources of Advice/Examples
1. Published review schedules	**Fully representative** Typically gathers views from *all* members of staff **Focus thinking and effort** Create their own momentum and encourage discussion and debate **Minimise preparation time** Usually provide pro-formas for immediate use **Offer a perspective on the whole school** Tend to explore many dimensions of school life and facilitate generalisation **Protect against manipulation of issues by senior staff** The schedule identifies main issues	**Intrusive/onerous** Member of staff may have no 'thought out' views on some issues and object to 'form-filling' **Can be seen as non-specific** Often do not seem relevant to the school, its particular problems and opportunities **Complex to administer and interpret** Time saved in preparation is often swallowed up by subsequent administrative support **Impose organising categories on the data** Represent the authors' perspectives and values **Identify 'inappropriate' areas for action** Reveal priorities to which senior management will not or cannot respond **Can be introspective** During the review period the school can seem to shut itself off from its environment	Guidelines for Review and Internal Development in Schools (GRIDS) 1. Abbot, R. *et al.* (1988) *GRIDS Secondary School Handbook* Longman 2. Abbot, R. *et al.* (1988) *GRIDS Primary School Handbook* Longman Oxfordshire County Council, Education Department (1979) *Starting Points in Self Evaluation* Cumming, J. (1986) *Evaluating your own school: a guide to action* Victoria Institute of Education Hopkins, D. (1988) *Doing School Based Review: Instruments and Guidelines* ACCO Hopkins, D. (1989) *Evaluation for School Development* Open University Press Elliott-Kemp, J. and Williams, G. L. (1980) *The DION Handbook* Pavic Publications

Figure 4.2 *Continued*

Method	Advantage	Limitations	Sources of Advice/Examples
2. Using audit matrices	**Versatility** Can be designed to gather information on a wide range of issues	**Indicative rather than diagnostic** Reveal *what* is happening not *why*	LEA Curriculum Audit Documents (see for example Bedfordshire Education Department (1990) *A Guide to Audits*)
	High staff involvement Potentially all members of staff can contribute to the data gathering exercise	**Temptation to 'cut corners'** Individuals can fill in what 'ought' to be happening rather than establishing what really is happening	National Curriculum Council (1990) *The Whole Curriculum* HMSO Hargreaves, *et al.* (1989) *Planning for School Development* HMSO
	Provide clear visual representation The matrix is a simple summative device which assists understanding and communication	**Address single issues** Usually a series of matrices will be needed where the issue is complex	Armitage, A. and Holden P. (1989) *TVEI Staff Development Manual 1* Framework Press See Appendix 1 for example of Curriculum Audit Charts
	Produce a neutral view Present a picture of the current situation as a basis for discussion rather than implying solutions	**Can be divisive** May reveal significant differences between teachers or departments	
	Quick and easy to devise Limit the amount of time needed for preparation work	**Need time to discuss** Teachers need time/opportunity to reflect on the information generated	

Figure 4.2 *Continued*

Method	Advantage	Limitations	Sources of Advice/Examples
3. Using staff meetings	**Can address specific issues/problems** Particular aspects of the school can be identified for analysis	**Difficult to maintain focus** Need careful chairing to be effective review bodies	Schmuck, R. and Runkel, P. (1985) *The Handbook of Organizational Development* Mayfield
	Gather a range of views Meetings can be representative of the spread of views and levels	**Personal recall** Individual's recall of events is often unreliable – accurate summaries/records are vital	Johnson, D. W. and Johnson, F. P. (1982) *Joining Together* Prentice Hall
			Miles, M. B. (1981) *Learning to Work in Groups* Teachers' College Press
	Foster debate amongst staff Allow exploration of causes and effects as well as establishing facts	**Can be divisive** Can increase differences in view between individuals and groups within the school	Rackham *et al.* (eds) (1971) *Developing Interactive Skills* Wellens
			Pemberton, M. (1982) *A Guide to Effective Meetings* The Industrial Society
	Increased morale Encourage staff to feel views are seen as valuable, increase levels of commitment and involvement	**Decreased morale** Can leave staff not involved feeling 'excluded' and under-valued	Warwick, D. (1982) *Effective Meetings* The Industrial Society
		Time consuming Need careful preparation Often disruptive or require staff to stay on for long periods after school	Hastings *et al.* (1986) *The Superteam Solution* Gower Press

Figure 4.2 *Continued*

Method	Advantage	Limitations	Sources of Advice/Examples
4. Using questionnaires	**Representative** All staff can be included in the review process **Specific** Can address particular areas of school life **Combine facts and opinions** Can gather information about what is happening and how staff feel about this **Minimise time needed for information collection** An appropriately designed questionnaire can solicit a quick, accurate response from staff **Can include other groups in the school's community** Parents, governors, LEA officers can contribute their views	**Preparation time** Questionnaires need careful planning and construction, and relevant expertise in design **Superficiality** Staff may feel that a questionnaire produces a shallow or misleading picture **Non-response** Some members of staff may fail to complete the questionnaire **Data analysis** The information produced by a questionnaire survey can be both too narrow (closed questions) and too diffuse (open questions) for sensible analysis	Bell, J. (1987) *Doing Your Research Project* Open University Press Youngman, M. B. (1986) *Analysing Questionnaires* University of Nottingham School of Education Cohen, L. and Manion, L. (1985) *Research Methods in Education* Croom-Helm Walker, R. (1985) *Doing Research: A Handbook for Teachers* Routledge Hopkins, D. (1985) *A Teacher's Guide to Classroom Research* Open University De Roche, E. F. (1981) *An Administrator's Guide for Evaluating Programs and Personnel* Allyn and Bacon

Figure 4.2 *Continued*

Method	Advantage	Limitations	Sources of Advice/Examples
5. Interviewing staff	**Representative** Interviews can be carried out with a range of staff from different areas and levels within the school **Quality of information** The interview format allows for collection of complex and high quality data **Relationships** The interview can increase mutual understanding and improve relationships between members of staff **Testing responses** The interview allows the interviewer to test out responses to possible actions or changes	**Time-consuming** Interviews are time-consuming both in terms of preparation and the time needed to carry them out **Status/credibility of interviewers** Some members of staff may be seen as inappropriate persons for this role, others may have insufficient influence **Consistency** Where more than one interviewer is involved it is difficult to guarantee a consistent approach – staff may be answering different questions **Information processing** Analysing and summarising interview data is a lengthy and difficult process	Wragg, E. C. (1980) *Conducting and Analysing Interviews* (Rediguide 11) University of Nottingham, School of Education Spradley, J. P. (1979) *The Ethnographic Interview* Holt, Rinehart and Winston Woods, P. (1986) *Inside Schools* Routledge Bell, J. (1987) *Doing Your Research Project* Open University Powney, J. and Watts, M. (1987) *Interviewing in Educational Research* Routledge

Figure 4.2 *Continued*

Method	Advantage	Limitations	Sources of Advice/Examples
6. Classroom observation	**Provides information on teacher behaviour** Allows access to data about teaching styles and approaches **Provides information on pupil response** Allows access to data about pupil attitudes and behaviours within the classroom **Stimulates reflection** Those being observed will tend to think hard about their own classroom practice **Feedback to teachers** It can be used to provide developmental feedback to teachers as well as to review pupil experiences **Benefits observers** Observing colleagues in action can be a powerful factor in personal development	**Focus restricted** Appropriate for reviewing only certain aspects of school life **Data recording and analysis** Data can be difficult to classify and summarise **Judgemental** It can be difficult to maintain a neutral stance rather than making judgements about what is being observed **Time-consuming** Classroom observation takes time to prepare and conduct **Threatening** Some teachers find the presence of another adult in the classroom disturbing **Distortion** The presence of an observer can change the normal pattern of classroom interaction	Croll, P. (1986) *Systematic Classroom Observation* Falmer Press Delamont, S. (1983) *Interaction in the Classroom* Methuen Flanders, N. (1970) *Analysing Teaching Behaviour* Addison Wesley Hopkins, D. (1985) *A Teacher's Guide to Classroom Research* Open University Press Hook, C. (1981) *Studying Classrooms* Deakin University Press Anderson, L. W. and Burns, R. B. (1989) *Research in Classrooms* Pergamon Acheson, K. and Gall, M. (1980) *Techniques in the Clinical Supervision of Teachers* Longman Galton, M. (1978) *British Mirrors* University of Leicester School of Education

Figure 4.2 *Continued*

Method	Advantage	Limitations	Sources of Advice/Examples
7. Analysing documentation	**Little additional effort or time to collect** Takes advantage of information which has already been produced	**Incomplete information** Information collected for other purposes will rarely wholly satisfy the needs of a review process	Woods, P. (1986) *Inside Schools* Routledge Cohen, L. and Manion, L. (1985) *Research Methods in Education* Croom Helm Bell, J. (1987) *Doing Your Research Project* Open University Press
	Offers insights into the culture of the school The content and style of documents can be most revealing	**Accuracy** Documents may not always be accurate or complete	Lincoln, Y. and Guba, E. (1985) *Naturalistic Inquiry* Sage
	Can identify changes/developments over time It is possible to trace developments back over a number of years	**Limited focus** Records and documents are only useful for certain types of enquiry	Open University (1981) *Course E364: Curriculum Evaluation and Assessment* Open University Press
	Can draw on external sources It is possible to explore aspects of the environment in which the school operates	**Time-consuming** Checking and analysing can be a lengthy job	Miles, M. B. and Huberman, A. M. (1984) *Qualitative Data Analysis* Sage

Figure 4.2 *Continued*

Method	Advantage	Limitations	Sources of Advice/Examples
8. Using 'outsiders'	**Impartiality** Outsiders will not be associated with particular areas of school performance **Different perspective** Outsiders will not necessarily share the assumptions and rationalisations which are present in the school's thinking **Informed view** Some outsiders, because of their own work, will have experiences and ideas which can be valuable to the school **Little demand on school resources** Normal work patterns largely unaffected	**Lack of 'local' knowledge** Outsiders may not be aware of the school's history, traditions, etc. **Personal agendas** Some of those who act as external consultants bring with them their own views and interests to promote **Credibility and trust** School staff will need to accept the 'competence' of the outsider used, and to feel secure about the process **Cost constraints** Some external consultants will need to be 'bought in' **Time-scales** Existing reviews by outsiders (e.g. Inspection) may not match the school's review schedule	Gray, H. L. (1988) *Management Consultancy in Schools* Cassell Stillman, A. and Grant, M. (1989) *The LEA Adviser – A Changing Role* NFER Nelson HMI/Scottish Education Department (1988) 1. *Effective Secondary Schools* HMSO 2. *Effective Primary Schools* HMSO Cabinet Office (1981) *Scrutiny of HM Inspectors of Schools in Scotland* Scottish Office Winkley, D. (1985) *Diplomats and Detectives LEA Advisers at Work* Robert Royce Becher et al. (1981) *Policies for Educational Accountability* Heinemann Millman, J. (ed) (1981) *Handbook of Teacher Evaluation* Sage Publications Pearce, J. (1986) *Standards and the LEA* NFER–Nelson

matrix analysis, e.g. teaching and learning opportunities, curriculum content and processes, staff experience and development needs.

Of course it is important to ensure that the matrix is completed by those with *actual information* about the area under review, as there are often significant differences between what we intend in schools and what actually happens. (As those who have carried pupil trails will no doubt appreciate!)

(iii) *Holding meetings*

Given that a review is likely to involve the need to gather information and views from a number of people, meetings have become an obvious way of working. Schools tend to have lots of meetings and, indeed, it is not uncommon to hear teachers complain about the amount of time these meetings take up. Consequently if meetings are to be a central strategy in the review it is important that they are conducted in ways that are purposeful and stimulating for participants, and cost effective.

Senior staff within a school have a particularly significant role to play in helping to make meetings successful. Their attitudes and behaviour are important in helping to create a positive feeling. They can do this by being sensitive to the views of their colleagues and by providing positive encouragement to all who participate. It is important to remember that the main purpose is to create an atmosphere in which individuals will feel able to make a contribution. (See Chapter 5).

If meetings are to be regarded as purposeful they should be arranged and conducted in a business-like manner. Experience has shown that the following steps can help:

(1) Participants should be provided with information about what is to be discussed beforehand in order that they can prepare their own ideas.

(2) Meetings should be seen to arrive at conclusions. Teachers tend to enjoy talking about their work and if discussions are not focused on some clear purpose they can become aimless.

(3) At the end of a meeting it is helpful if conclusions and/or decisions are summarised.

(4) Where appropriate after a meeting, conclusions and/or decisions should be written up and each participant issued with a copy.

Meetings in schools can have negative effects on teacher attitudes and morale if participants feel uncomfortable or unenthusiastic about the ways in which they are conducted. For example, individuals may be embarrassed if they feel that they are likely to appear foolish in front of colleagues. Others may lose interest when meetings are seen to be meandering or are dominated by one or two contributors. The aim should be to make meetings as enjoyable and effective as possible.

(iv) *Using questionnaires*

On the surface the use of questionnaires seems to provide a relatively simple and straightforward means of gathering information quickly from large groups of people. Experience suggests, however, that it is an approach that can be fraught with difficulties. Too often the questionnaires that are used have been poorly designed and, as a consequence, fail to provide the quality of information that is required. If a questionnaire is to be used as a review vehicle it is worthwhile to invest time finding out a little more about questionnaire design.

Questionnaires may include closed or open-ended questions. However it has to be said that open-ended questions often produce such unforeseen responses that the information collected may prove difficult or even impossible to analyse. Generally the most effective questionnaires consist of questions for which the form of response that is required is clearly defined.

The main issues that need to be considered in questionnaire construction are: question content, question wording, forms of response and the sequencing of items. On all these matters it makes sense to carry out some form of piloting before using the questionnaires fully.

(v) *Interviewing staff*

In simple terms an interview is merely a conversation aimed at gathering information. It can take many forms and it is this variety that is one of its greatest strengths. Different forms of interviews can be used depending upon the nature of the information that is being sought and taking account of contextual factors and constraints.

Interviews may be short or long; they can be highly structured based upon a predetermined set of questions or loosely focused; they may involve individuals or groups of people. The great advantage is that unexpected comments can be pursued and responses that are unclear can be clarified by further discussion.

In planning interviews the following issues need to be considered:

● who should be interviewed

- the format of the questions to be asked
- the creation of an appropriate context
- how responses are to be recorded.

Preparation is vital if the interview is to generate reliable information.

(vi) *Observing classrooms*

Inevitably a review of school policy is likely to include some consideration of classroom practice. Finding ways of gathering information about what goes on in classrooms is not easy, however. There is a tradition of privacy amongst teachers which means that visits from 'outsiders' are viewed with suspicion. Further, the presence of an observer tends to distort the natural environment of the classroom making it difficult for normal activity to be observed. Finally, at a methodological level, the complexities of the classroom make it difficult for the observer to decide what to focus upon.

All of this assumes, of course, that somebody can be found who has the time to spend observing classroom life. Certainly there is much to be gained in terms of professional development in finding ways of enabling colleagues to observe one another at work. Regrettably teachers have little opportunity to observe practice and yet there is considerable evidence to suggest that this can be a powerful means of helping individuals to reflect upon and develop their own teaching (e.g. Joyce and Showers, 1988; Bradley *et al.*, 1989; West and Bollington, 1990.).

Another possibility is for teachers to collect information themselves about their own practice. This idea is consistent with the views put forward by Schon (1983), who has suggested that improvements in professional practice can best be achieved by encouraging 'reflection-in action'. In other words, teachers should be attempting to analyse their own approaches with a view to finding ways of developing their own practice. Some writers (e.g. Hopkins, 1985; Stenhouse, 1975) suggest that various forms of audio-visual recording may be helpful in providing information that can help teachers to review aspects of their classroom behaviour.

Certainly there is an extensive literature on classroom observation and much which could be adapted to generate information relevant to school review. Once again, as with other methods, observation can vary in style from, at one extreme, highly structured approaches using predetermined schedules, to much more open approaches that use various forms of narrative or 'free' recording.

(vii) *Analysing documents*

Documents may provide a further source of relevant information that can inform the process of review. These may include national or local authority policy documents, school documents or examples of children's written work.

Bell (1987) suggests the following agenda for analysing documents:

- What kind of document is it?
- What does it actually say?
- Who provided it? What was its purpose?
- How did it come into existence?
- Is it typical or exceptional of its type?
- Is it complete? Has it been altered or edited?

At the present time it may well be worth reviewing 'public' documents which represent the school – it is vital to consider the impression such documents will make on governors and parents as well as the quality of information they include.

There is also a wealth of data in most schools which has not been formally 'documented', but which can contribute significantly to a review process. For example, patterns of subject choice by pupils, or examination results, especially viewed over time, can reveal trends and help to establish baselines.

(viii) *Using 'outsiders'*

A further strategy for gathering information as part of a review may be to use someone external to the school. Inspectors, advisory teachers, representatives from higher education and governors could be particularly helpful in this respect. Inevitably they would draw upon one or other of the approaches described above to collect their information. Perhaps their most valuable asset, however, is that they have the ability to look at the school, or some aspect of its practice, from a different perspective. They may also bring to their work experiences of practice in other schools that can help staff to see things in a different way.

If it is the intention to use an outsider as part of the review process it is important that they are well briefed as to the background and purpose of the review. Care must also be taken to address diplomatic and ethical issues that arise as a result of somebody visiting the school in a manner that seems to be judgemental. The potential benefits of an outside view are such that it may be worth exploring possibilities, and the involvement of governors in such an exercise can be particularly beneficial, bringing dividends beyond those associated with the review itself.

Checking the information

Given that most forms of enquiry involve other people, their behaviour and their points of view, it is important to consider the ethical implications of the review process. As a matter of principle, it is vital that the individual rights of those involved should be protected, whether they are colleagues, pupils or parents. On a more pragmatic level, the future of any development that is to be successful will also depend upon the good-will of everybody involved.

Elliott (1981) suggests that the key ethical issues to bear in mind relate to confidentiality, negotiation and control. He argues that confidential information should not be released until this has been agreed with the person or persons to whom it belongs. In carrying out a review within a school, therefore, a code of ethics that addresses these sorts of issues should be determined and this should be made clear to everybody who is likely to be involved.

A related issue concerns the questions of trustworthiness with respect to information that is gathered as part of the review process. In other words, how can we persuade others that these findings are worthy of attention? In particular:

● Does the method used measure or describe what it set out to do? (i.e. is it *valid*?)
● Does the method provide similar information on different occasions? (i.e. is it *reliable*?)

Where the investigation is 'one-off' it is usually impossible to be certain about the answers to these questions but, nevertheless, they should be borne in mind.

A particular strategy used for checking information and, in so doing, giving authority to the findings, is known as triangulation. Put simply this means the use of two or more sets of information to study the one event or process. It may, for example, involve comparing and contrasting information using different methods (e.g. interviews and observation) or by comparing and contrasting the views of different people. There is a range of other methods for checking the trustworthiness of methods that may also be appropriate. Useful sources of advice include Cohen and Manion (1985), Elliott (1981), Lincoln and Guba (1985), Miles and Huberman (1984) and Skrtic (1985). The important point here is that the quality and reliability of information collected during a review process is likely to increase if a range of methods is used.

Making sense of the information

Having gathered together various forms of information the next step must be to make sense of it. This stage in the review is sometimes referred to as data analysis. The way in which this is carried out will be determined to a large extent by the nature of the information itself. In general terms, the issue is clear. What we are seeking is a framework that allows us to organise and structure the information and share it with others in order to illuminate, interpret and explain the area of policy that is under consideration.

Often the purpose and scope of the review provides a framework for analysing the information that has been collected. Usually this will indicate questions or headings against which the data may be analysed. For example, Hargreaves *et al.* (1989) suggest a format that schools might use when reviewing the curriculum with respect to the requirements of the Education Reform Act and the National Curriculum. The format proposes that schools should carry out a review in order to:

- check whether the planned curriculum meets the statutory requirements;
- identify possible gaps or overlap between subject areas;
- ensure that where two or more subjects or activities are concerned with the same range of objectives, this is recognised and used positively;
- analyse the curriculum for each year group in terms of curricular objectives within and outside the National Curriculum;
- decide in which parts of the school curriculum to locate work leading to the National Curriculum and other school curricular objectives;
- assess how much teaching time is available and how best to use it;
- compare *planned* provision with *actual* provision;
- judge whether curriculum issues need to be among the priorities for development.

Clearly these headings could be used as a set of categories against which review information could be assembled in order to facilitate analysis and interpretation.

When information of a statistical nature has been gathered – such as assessment or examination results, for example – the analysis may well be relatively straight-forward. Simple procedures for processing and presenting this type of data are well documented (e.g. Campbell and Stanley, 1963). Overall the aim here should be to present the findings in ways that can make them accessible to a wide audience. Often visual representations such as graphs and flow-charts can be helpful in this respect.

However, much of the information gathered may by its nature be much more difficult to process. In particular, when large amounts of qualitative data have been collected, within structures that are relatively open-ended, the issues can be complex. Having said that, it is also worth adding that this type of information is often the most valuable in terms of informing the planning approach. Furthermore, the process of engaging with the data in order to make sense of it may well be a valuable intellectual exercise for those involved, leading them to have greater insights into the issues with which they are concerned.

Ainscow and Conner (1990) suggest a series of five stages that can help groups of people to make sense of data that they are collecting as part of an inquiry. These are: reduction, explanation, interpretation, critique and reporting. We will consider these in turn.

(i) *Data reduction*

This is the preliminary stage of the process of analysis, an attempt to make sense of the material gathered. This may go on both during and following the collection of the data. The aim is to organise the information in relation to themes or patterns which emerge, and significant events or comments that appear particularly important. The themes or patterns may have been there at the outset of the review or they may have evolved as it was carried out. In part this is a filtering process in order to make decisions about what is important and what can be rejected. As Powney and Watts (1987) suggest:

> ...part of the creative process in analysis is to impose a structure on the accumulated material...Judgements are made at every point as to what material is relevant and what is irrelevant...Deliberate selection is necessary at all stages...Much material is therefore lost.

Bogden and Biklen (1982) offer advice about analysis when doing research, some of which is pertinent to the early stages of the review process. They suggest:

(1) *Force yourself to make decisions that narrow the inquiry*
     You must discipline yourself not to pursue everything ... or else you

are likely to wind up with data too diffuse and inappropriate for what you decide to do. The more data you have on a given topic, setting, or subjects, the easier it will be to think deeply about it and the more productive you are likely to be when you attempt the final analysis.

(2) *Force yourself to make decisions concerning the type of inquiry you want to conduct*
You should try to make clear in your own mind, for example, whether you want to do a full description of a setting or whether you are interested in a particular aspect of it.

(3) *Develop analytic questions*
Some researchers bring general questions to a study. These are important because they give focus to data collection and help organise it as you proceed . . . We suggest that shortly after you enter the field, you assess which questions you brought with you are relevant and which ones should be reformulated to direct your work.

(4) *Plan data collection sessions according to what you find in previous observations*
In light of what you find when you periodically review your field notes, plan to pursue specific leads in your data collection session.

(5) *Write memos to yourself about what you are learning*
The idea is to stimulate critical thinking about what you see and to become more than a recording machine.

(6) *Try out ideas and themes on colleagues*
While not everyone should be asked, and while not all you hear may be helpful, key informants, under the appropriate circumstances, can help advance your analysis, especially to fill in the holes in description.

Some further practical ideas are outlined by Goetz and Le Compte (1984) who suggests the following steps to help reduce the data to more manageable proportions:

● Review the original purpose underlying the review. Although this might have changed, it reminds you of the audience for whom the study was originally intended.
● Read through all the data several times, jotting down notes, comments, observations, queries in a margin. The production of a separate running list of major ideas that cut across these may also be helpful.

● Use notes to develop a primitive outline or system of categorisation.
● Transform the patterns and regularities into categories which will aid future analysis.

(ii) *Explanation*

Having undertaken the reduction of the data the next stage begins the process of explaining the analysis. Here the aim is to introduce the audience, whoever it is intended they may be, to the issues that have been identified as of central importance. At this stage it is likely to be in the form of a description of the significant issues that have emerged. Often the most useful way of presenting the analysis is in some kind of narrative form, but using graphs, charts, tables and breakdowns of the analysis as averages of percentages offers a helpful means of making the information more undertakeable and accessible.

Watts (1983) provides a useful rule of thumb for the number of issues to be addressed at the explanation stage. He suggests a 'seven-plus-or-minus-two' rule to indicate the number of categories that might suitably arise from a data source. This suggests that if there are more than ten categories then the analysis is becoming unwieldly; if there are fewer than four then it raises questions about the extent to which the data has been carefully scrutinised.

(iii) *Interpretation*

Running alongside, and often inextricably linked with the explanation stage is an attempt to offer interpretations as to *why* particular issues are seen as being significant. This may involve comparing and contrasting the findings with those of others reported in relevant books or journals. It may also lead to going beyond the information collected in order to collect more data that can confirm or reject a hypothesis that has emerged.

At this stage the issues of reliability and validity referred to earlier will again have to be addressed. As Miles (1979) notes,

> ...the analyst faced with a bank of qualitative data has very few guidelines for protection against self-delusion let alone the presentation of 'unreliable' or 'invalid' conclusions... How can we be sure that an 'earthy', 'undeniable', 'serendipitous' finding is not, in fact, wrong?

Reflecting upon this question and attempting to offer evidence to support any claims made is an essential feature of this stage of the review process.

Conclusions emerge and are strengthened over time. At first, the noting of regularities, patterns, explanations is done tentatively and with some scepticism. As the analysis progresses, however, conclusions become increasingly explicit, with corroborative and substantial evidence to support the findings, both from the data itself and other sources.

(iv) *Critique*

On completion of the analysis, there is a need to stand back from it in order to reflect critically upon its appropriateness to the original intentions. This is, in practice, a further attempt at verification of the findings before coming to final conclusions. Verification can be carried in the following ways:

● Revisiting the data and scanning it for second thoughts or alternative explanations. Is there anything of importance being missed? Are there any negative instances that seem to contradict the findings?

● Feeding back the emerging interpretations to colleagues for their reactions. How does the interpretation seem to them? Have their comments been dealt with honestly?

● Looking for other ways of testing the plausibility of the findings of the review. Do they stand up to the critical scrutiny of others outside the review?

● Considering whether the findings can be confirmed by evidence outside the data that has been collected. Are there other sources of information which can be consulted?

(v) *Reporting*

If the review has been conducted by an individual or small group its findings may well have to be presented to a wider audience, possibly the whole staff. Walker (1985) suggests that the onus of selecting non-technical and non-threatening ways to present the findings of such a report lies firmly on the writer. He mentions oral delivery, audio-visual displays, and novel literacy forms as well as the conventional report. His advice is to analyse the 'context of use' of the findings and to ask pertinent questions about the audience and purposes the review is intended to serve.

The handling of this reporting stage is crucial if the aim is to encourage colleagues to participate in any plans that emerge as a result of the review process. Consequently care should be taken to make it meaningful, relevant and interesting. This being the case, the following points should be kept in mind.

The presentation of review information should be:

● brief, giving the necessary information in forms that are easy to digest;
● focused, allowing the intended audience to see the most important issues and themes;
● fair, in providing an even-handed account, including contradictory information or views where they exist;
● free of jargon, in order that everybody can feel comfortable with the information that is presented;
● clear in making distinctions between facts and interpretations.

Finally it is helpful to set out the alternatives for action in order that those involved can begin to address the issues in a constructive manner.

Summary

The focus in this chapter is the question 'What happens at present?', and how a school might look for answers. Suggestions have been made as to how appropriate methods for collecting together and analysing information can be determined in order that subsequent planning is based on an accurate picture of where the school is currently. Stress has also been placed on the need to check this information with respect to trustworthiness and the need for care in reporting it to colleagues.

Our own view is that though there are published review schedules available, these will rarely coincide with actual needs. Schools should therefore seek to combine a variety of approaches to review and be prepared to 'alter' and 'redesign' as appropriate. Confidence can be built via *the way information is processed, analysed and reported* rather than the particular techniques used to gather it.

CHAPTER FIVE

From Review to Planning

The planning process

The information gathered during the review process, when interpreted in the light of national and local requirements and the school's own objectives and context, will provide a picture of strengths and weaknesses. In consultation with the school's governors, this picture needs to be developed into a plan (or series of plans) which identifies targets for the coming year and indicates how resources will be deployed in pursuit of these targets (Figure 5.1).

Of course, much of what the school hopes to achieve in the next year will relate to continuity – projecting current strengths into the future. Some targets will emerge from areas of weakness; there will always be some areas of performance where things did not turn out quite as hoped or unforeseen circumstances frustrated efforts. There will also probably be scope for new policies – opportunities to pursue new objectives rather

Figure 5.1   The efficiency cycle

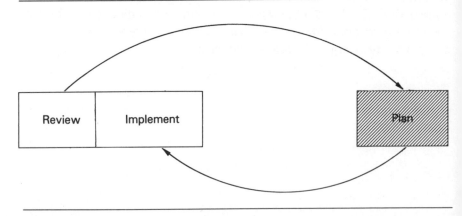

than maintain existing ones or remedy areas of concern. Planning can therefore be seen as a process which seeks to:

- maintain current levels of performance across a number of areas of activity;
- improve levels of performance in one or two areas where results have been disappointing and objectives have not been realised;
- establish new objectives/develop new areas of activity which increase the overall quality of the school's performance.

Of course, some balance of emphasis between these three areas will be necessary. One difficulty of encouraging teachers to identify developmental activities which they see as necessary or desirable is that this will often result in a much longer list of new objectives than the school is able to resource. It may also deflect attention away from current activities which need effort if they are to be maintained. Nevertheless, this essentially 'deficit-based' approach (What are we *not* doing?) has been common at both school and LEA levels, and perhaps accounts for the disappointing impact of many self-evaluation approaches, as well as explaining widespread dissatisfaction with LEA policies on staff-development.

Similarly, it may be possible to 'overlook' areas where little progress has been achieved despite the targeting of effort and resources, and to argue for different objectives rather than different (and more successful) approaches to the same objective. At the core of the planning process therefore is the need to make judgements. In the light of information generated by review/audit processes and informed by the school's objectives, school governors and senior staff will need to be able to identify priorities both across and within the three broad areas, i.e.

- priorities for maintenance
- priorities for improvement
- priorities for development

They will also need to ensure that the balance between the areas is one which can be resourced and which promotes *long term* school development.

The School Development Plans Project Report (Hargreaves *et al.*, 1989) suggested that this involves a number of stages:

- determining priorities for development
- constructing and agreeing on the plan
- publicising the plan
- drawing up action plans
- linking the development plan with other aspects of planning.

This is a useful description, as it emphasises the need both to *identify priorities* at the beginning of the planning process and to *integrate* the different aspects of planning, though perhaps the stress on 'development' underestimates the extent to which schools will need to focus on maintenance issues. It also underlines the need to describe plans in terms of the *actions* which must take place if they are to be realised. Unless priorities can be closely related to real tasks it will be difficult either to focus effort or to estimate how successful the school has been.

It can be helpful here to remember that in translating priorities into specific objectives, a number of dimensions need to be built in.

Time   Plans must be time-related: it is necessary to decide *when* we expect to see particular objectives achieved.

Quality   Some method of measuring the 'quality' of outcome required is important; the aim should be to establish acceptable quality standards which are realistic.

Quantity Similarly it is important to consider the level or amount of activity which should be related to the particular objective.

Cost   A clear indication of the resources which will be directed towards securing the objective should be given to those involved.

Thus, statements such as 'to ensure that proper attention is paid to cross curricular themes' are, as mentioned previously, forecasts rather than plans, and are not especially helpful to the staff who are expected to ensure that this priority is met. Efforts should be made to establish a form of expressing plans which incorporates the dimensions listed above and communicates these clearly to those involved.

Thus: 'to ensure that all courses offered within year ten select one cross curricular theme to target during the next year, and that each theme is targeted in at least *two* curricular areas. To review progress at the end of the year', gives a clear indication of timescale, level of activity and cost limits (i.e. it is to be done within existing resources). Quality indicators are often more difficult to build into planning statements. Sometimes quality and quantity are related – the more we hope to achieve the lower the quality standard which can be met. Frequently, the closest we can get to 'quality' in the short term is to monitor implementation, rather than evaluate outcomes. It is possible nevertheless to identify criteria, which could be approached either by deciding to audit inputs, e.g. reviewing how and where particular themes have been tackled by the curricular areas, or by gathering data about impact, e.g. devising some way of checking pupils' understanding of the themes at the end of the year.

Planning systems

There are approaches which can help incorporate these dimensions but without making them explicit. In local government, Planning, Programming, Budgeting Systems (PPBS) were developed to meet this need, seeking to provide an approach which links planning into action and provides for monitoring and resource control through four stages (GLC 1972, quoted in Stewart, 1974):

Planning
Assessing needs, establishing priorities, setting objectives, and choosing the means of attaining them from the available alternatives.

Programming
Organising and controlling specific courses of action in relation to the objectives they serve and presenting them in a performance and resources use plan over a period of years.

Budgeting
Translating planning and programming decisions into specific financial plans for a relatively short period of time (one year).

System
Integrating, checking and reviewing all planning, programming and budgeting decisions within a consistent framework of general management.

This approach encouraged planners to think about timescales, levels of activity (both required and feasible) and the resource (cost) implications of particular activities. 'Checking and reviewing' enables the quality of decisions as well as the quality of implementation of decisions to be monitored.

Stewart (*op. cit.*) also argued that such approaches brought with them certain characteristics which demonstrated the advantages to a local authority of a corporate approach to planning when compared with incremental or fragmentary procedures. These advantages, if they can be realised, would bring significant benefits to schools.

There was a movement towards *explicit policymaking*, for example, rather than a perception of policy as something which emerged from an analysis of activities. The audit or review process provided a description of current policies which had not necessarily been available previously. It was able to make explicit links between objectives, roles and activities, and to underline the factors which had contributed to particular decisions. This was often accompanied by a movement towards *systematic policy review and analysis*, and again it seems likely that the school which begins to articulate actual policies will be drawn into policy analysis in at least some areas, rather than finding comfort in the (often vague) statements of educational intent which are a feature of so many school brochures.

Stewart also detected an *increased concern for environmental analysis* – those making decisions within the organisation became aware of the need for information about the environment in which the organisation was operating. Thus finding out more about the *felt* needs of pupils, parents, governors and communities would become a pre-requisite for improving decision-making and increasing the effectiveness of the school.

Explicit identification of objectives was a further benefit – organisations adopting a corporate approach to planning tended to focus on purposes rather than activities in the first instance. This often encouraged debate about different ways of achieving the same objective, rather than a narrow defence of existing activities which may or may not contribute to overall effectiveness. Indeed, the very creation of a series of objectives for the whole organisation seemed to stimulate discussion of the *contribution of different groups to the same objective*. This should be a crucial factor in school planning, both because of the cumulative nature of many educational objectives, and because the division of the school into groupings, though inevitable for administrative and organisational purposes, should not lead us to overlook the continuous nature of schooling as experienced by the pupil.

Finally, Stewart identified an increasing *concern for output measurement*, which has become as apparent in education in recent years as it was in the parallel period of local government reform about which he is writing. He adds wrily:

> The word used is 'concern' because there has been more expression of concern for output measures than has been achieved.

Those who have followed the debates concerning examination reform, national testing and performance indicators may well sympathise with his observation here, but it seems inevitable that output measures of various kinds will be applied both within and without the school, and if a systematic approach to planning and review stimulates thinking in this area, it is likely to improve the school's ability to identify and to project what it does best.

The PPBS approach also highlighted the scope of corporate planning: programmes are needed in a number of areas and these programmes need to be coordinated. The planning process will need therefore to integrate these different strands.

But despite the benefits Stewart associated with this approach, PPBS has not generally been considered successful as a technique for planning, rather than a method of conceptualising the planning process. It seems that the advantages it offers are outweighed by difficulties of implementing such an approach. Caldwell and Spinks (1988) offer some explanation of these difficulties.

> There is now a general recognition that PPBS failed for reasons which included excessive attentions to the minutiae of budgeting, the excessive paperwork, lack of flexibility, the lack (at that time) of effective low-cost computer based accounting and management information systems, and timelines for implementation which were unrealistic. To these short-comings may be added an inappropriate emphasis on the specification of performance requirements or criteria for evaluation.

The message here is clear; vital as the planning process is, we need to remember that a planning system is there to serve the organisation, not find ourselves modifying the organisation to serve the planning system, Caldwell and Spinks go on to suggest how this might be tackled, using Collaborative School Management (CSM).

Collaborative School Management is outlined as an approach which links planning into implementation through six stages:

- Goal setting and need identification
- Policy making, which is divided into defining purposes and establishing broad guidelines
- Programme planning
- Preparation and agreement of programme budgets
- Implementing programmes
- Evaluating the impact of programmes.

The first two stages in this cycle are carried out by the senior management team or 'policy group' in the school. The remaining stages are devolved to a variety of 'programme groups', which could be teaching departments or other functional groupings. Caldwell and Spinks argue that this will create 'involvement' in the planning process by the teachers who make up the programme groups, so that unlike PPBS, teachers will be shaping rather than fitting into the programmes.

This is an attractive proposition, since clearly the extent to which teachers contribute to planning is likely to impact on performance. Further, they offer evidence (including 'excessive attention to the minutiae of budgeting') of how the approach has been applied in Rosebery District High School, Tasmania, to serve these outcomes.

Their distancing of Collaborative School Management from PPBS however is, in the end, unconvincing. Like PPBS, CSM provides a very useful model for thinking about corporate or whole school planning but its application as a *technique* seems no more (or less) likely to succeed, since both will flourish where the majority of staff have significant interest and involvement in policy-making and planning activities.

But the level of commitment, involvement and effort required to develop and maintain the system itself is likely to be difficult to engender in many schools, and hard to sustain where it takes hold.

Nonetheless, there are aspects of CSM which can be very usefully drawn on within the planning process. The need to establish a 'policy for policy-making', for example, is a very important notion, and the use of a standard format for programme objectives and budgets is also likely to prove beneficial.

Functions within planning

But the key question remains how best to 'divide' the planning process so that it is manageable and seems to reflect teachers working lives and concerns, whilst maintaining coherence. It is this combination of 'loose–tight properties' noted by Peters and Waterman (1982) which seems to characterise the effective organisation – a combination of 'firm central direction and maximum individual autonomy'.

Figure 5.2   Basic functions involved in planning

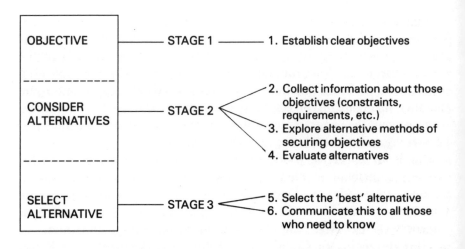

Figure 5.3   Coherence and the planning process

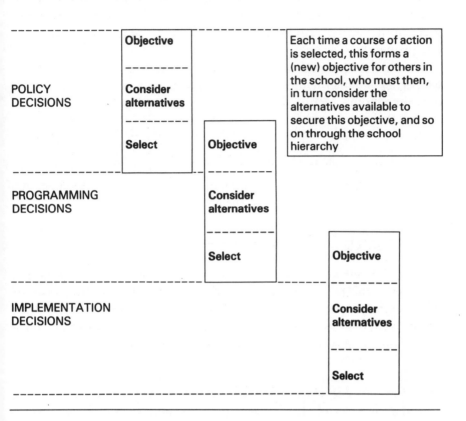

What we are seeking, then, are specific ideas on how the planning process can be decentralised yet coordinated without requiring large amounts of activity or volumes of paperwork to maintain or control the process. Let us, since we are looking for a solution which is realistic and as uncomplicated as is possible, return to the basic functions involved in planning. These can be summarised as shown in Figure 5.2

These functions can be carried out at a variety of levels within the school. What is important is that the *formulation of objectives is at a level appropriate to the nature of the objective*. The school, then, can be seen as an organisation in which the functions of planning are widespread (loose) but focused (tight) through a hierarchy of objectives (see Figure 5.3).

Each level in the school, in selecting from available methods of securing objectives, establishes objectives for the next level down, though the exploration and evaluation of alternatives (Stage 2) can be carried out by cross-hierarchical groups of staff. It is the school's *objective setting structure* which establishes control (as mentioned previously, via ideas) and not the school's organisation structure (by trying to limit or direct behaviour)

What we need to bear in mind however is that developing 'loose–tight' properties is much to do with the organisation's culture, creating an environment in which:

> The discipline (a few shared values) provides the framework. It gives people confidence (to experiment for instance) stemming from stable expectations about what really counts. (Peters and Waterman, *op. cit.*)

We see this as a central issue in school management and development and will return to this theme later in the chapter.

Areas where plans are required

Within this model, it seems sensible to recognise that specific sets of objectives will be needed in the different areas of the school's activity. Though the schools may vary in their needs, it seems likely that most schools will need plans related to the curriculum, to staffing policies and to resource acquisition and use. It may therefore be sensible to start by producing plans in each of these areas, refining each in light of possibilities presented and constraints imposed by the others. If the audit/revew process has been thorough then all will benefit from starting with the same information base. The Curriculum Plan is, of course, the most important expression of the school's responsibilities, objectives and values, but it needs to be developed in light of and in harmony with staffing and financial resources available. It can therefore be seen as both leading the planning process in those two areas, and responding to developments, opportunities and problems arising from those areas.

Figure 5.4 shows the relationships between the apparently discrete areas where plans are needed. The shaded area indicates the 'feasible area' for immediate action: it shows the extent to which the curriculum plan can be implemented through existing staff and resources. We have previously described this as predominantly *'maintaining'* aspects of the present curriculum, though it could of course include some areas where existing staff skills or resources can readily be redeployed into priority areas.

The unshaded portions of the plans represent the major *development* areas. At present, these plans do not affect implementation, as they are

Figure 5.4   Co-ordinating planning activity

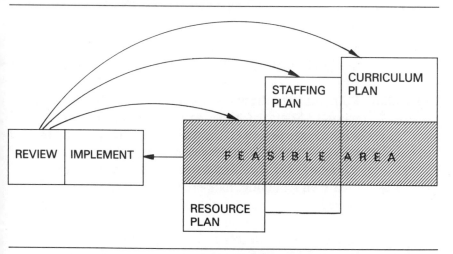

essentially preparatory: they indicate the developments required in order to extend the feasible area before the next planning period.

There may, for example, be

● a commitment to develop a course in a particular area (curriculum plan);
● the training of one or more teachers to work with new materials (staffing plan); or
● the remodelling of a teaching space (resource plan).

Such developments must be *planned and coordinated*, so that curriculum plans not realisable this year become major developments in future years.

Only one link into the 'implementation' stage is shown since, though it is possible to plan in discrete categories, it is rarely possible to act in discrete categories. Implementation is unity, it combines aspects of curriculum, staff and resource planning. Reviewing outcomes will however have implications for each area of planning.

Advice on planning in each of these areas is available, though not in equal proportions. Much has been written about the curriculum planning process, some about staff planning, little about resources. We offer some comments on each.

The curriculum plan

Governors and headteachers will need to work together on the production of the school's curriculum plan. Whitaker (1983) has suggested that curriculum planning activity needs to take account of at least four factors:

Prescription Meeting statutory requirements placed on schools, such as the implementation of the National Curriculum and of national policies on testing.

Expectation Responding to the many and varied expectations placed on schools. Some of these are rooted in convention and educational practice, i.e. they relate to the values and beliefs of teachers. Others arise from public perceptions of schooling, i.e. they are based on adults' recollections of their own schooling, tempered to a greater or lesser degree by information and publicity about educational issues. Increasingly important are expectations which relate to employment prospects and to employers.

Situation Reflecting the school's physical, social and educational environments. The attitudes and preferences of parents and the skills, attitudes and abilities of teachers are particularly important contextual factors. Devolution has seen the school's facilities and state of repair of school buildings receive considerable attention of late.

Predilection Developing a vision of what that school might become and recognising that without appropriate management actions this vision will never be realised. Curriculum development needs teacher development, and teacher development needs to be managed.

The School Development Plans Project Report (Hargreaves *et al.*, 1989) also starts with prescription, but then suggests a different emphasis within the curriculum planning process.

- Using a curriculum audit to improve the curriculum as a whole (breadth, balance, differentiation, relevance)
- Ensuring continuity and progression in the curriculum experienced by pupils
- Modifying the curriculum for a particular year group as appropriate.

If these values are to be built into the school's curriculum planning activity, then there will need to be a series of criteria which are used to assess the quality of the plan. A recent report by HM Inspectors (HMI/Scottish Education Department, 1988) provides useful suggestions which can form the basis of a checklist here:

  (i)   clarity of statements/guidelines;
 (ii)   consonance with school aims;
(iii)   consonance with national and regional guidelines;
(iv)   relationship to local and particular circumstances;
 (v)   design and organisation of courses at the various stages;
(vi)   overall breadth, balance and choice;
(vii)   match between curriculum and assessment, for example the extent
        to which assessment procedures have been analysed and selected to
        match curricular objectives;
(viii) recognition of individual needs and special educational needs; and
        the
(ix)   contribution of the informal curriculum and extra-curricular
        activities.

Once curriculum plans have been drawn up, and they have been
evaluated in terms of relevant educational criteria selected by the school,
those which are adopted will have direct influence on staff deployment
and development decisions.

The staffing plan

The staff plan can be seen as having two elements: first, indicating how
those activities required to implement the curriculum plan (maintenance)
will be covered; and second, showing what staff development activities
will be undertaken in the coming year.

It is important, where possible, to extend the principle of
'empowerment' to decisions about implementation. Where there are
groups of staff who, between them, will be required to cover sections or
areas of the curriculum plan, it makes sense to delegate decisions about
who will do what to the manager of the group (who may well decide to
involve the group members themselves). This approach – which means
that 'maintenance' decisions can be de-centralised, with the senior
management role becoming one of advice and coordination rather than
day-to-day involvement in staffing decisions – can promote a number of
healthy employment practices, such as:

Job enrichment The opportunity to be given greater respon-
                    sibility/autonomy discretion over the way tasks are
                    carried out.
Job rotation   The opportunity to take on different tasks within a
                    department or group – working with different aspects
                    of the subject or different groups of pupils.

Job enlargement The opportunity to build variety into tasks which particular teachers carry out, without requiring increases in teacher skills.

Of course, such an approach requires some knowledge of what individual teachers have done and can do, as well as what their current tasks are. A major blockage to teacher development is the apparent inflexibility of the time-table as a staff utilisation device; we need to be much more aware of the experience and abilities of colleagues (see Appendix 2 for an example of how this information can be collected and used) and much more creative in the ways we consider using them. This may mean relying less on INSET for overall development, though of course it will still have a vital and strategic role.

The INSET component of the staffing plan – the development plan – is well covered in the School Development Plans Project Report (Hargreaves *et al.*, 1989). It should involve:

- working out the INSET implications of key issue emerging from the audit;
- planning the INSET needed in relation to priorities and targets;
- checking that the relevant INSET can be provided;
- using INSET resources effectively where they have been delegated to the school by the LEA;
- matching the needs of the school with the professional development of individual teachers;
- ensuring that INSET opportunities are allocated fairly among the staff over time;
- ensuring that knowledge and skills acquired through INSET are disseminated within the school;
- evaluating the success of INSET in realising the development plan.

It must be remembered however, that most staff development takes place within the job. INSET funds are severely limited, and cannot hope to do more than stimulate and support the wider processes of personal development. The way staff are deployed within the school, and how this deployment is reinforced by interaction with colleagues and by increasing scope and responsibility within the job will be important features of the teacher's professional growth, the school's development. The staffing plan is therefore a vital aspect of the school's planning activity.

The resource plan

As indicated above, advice on resource planning in schools is not abundant. Everard and Morris (1985) suggested a number of issues related to resource control which may provide start points:

- Does the school know what resources it has and where these are by carrying out regular checks?
- Is there someone clearly responsible for the control and maintenance of each item of equipment?
- Does the school regularly review the uses to which resources are being put?

These are useful questions, and clearly any resource plan would need to address these areas, though a more fundamental question relating to what we classify as resources could probably be added to the list.

Several writers (see Davies, 1989, McAlister and Connolly, 1990), subsume resource planning issues within the wider context of budgetary planning for the school, and we see the logic of this approach. Our own view, however, is that the budget should more properly be regarded as the translation of all the school's plans, curriculum, staffing and resource, into financial plans and targets. Therefore we advocate a separate stage, when the ways in which non-staff resources can best be used to support the school's purposes are considered and decisions are made. This stage seems all the more important if the 'choices', which Torrington and Weightman (1989) suggest confront school managers, are to be tackled sensibly:

- making better use of what is available;
- raising additional resources, through PTAs, local businesses etc.
- doing less than they would like;
- cutting corners on the quality of what they do.

Clearly schools will come under increasing pressure to use, and to demonstrate that they are using resources optimally. Difficult choices about how best to allocate scarce resources amongst competing demands are therefore inevitable and school managers will need to develop the appropriate skills. To some extent, having clear curriculum priorities and development plans for the school simplifies matters, as these begin to provide criteria against which alternative resource use can be judged. But the school will also need some criteria for assessing the quality of the school's resource plan. Simkins and Lancaster (1987) offer criteria for assessing budgetary planning systems which are helpful here. Can the resource plan

(i) Respond equitably to the needs of different subject areas?
(ii) Enable priorities to be taken into account?

    (iii)   Promote organisational objectives?
    (iv)   Encourage innovation?
    (v)   Facilitate long-term planning?
    (vi)   Be easily understood?
    (vii)   Be widely accepted within the organisation?

What must be remembered is that *techniques* for resource planning, like techniques for staff or curriculum planning, will be beneficial only if the school has a pattern of organisation which can harness technique within a culture which knows how to use approaches rather than become subservient to them. As we noted earlier in the chapter, the measure of effective planning is appropriate results, not increasingly sophisticated planning procedures. We will therefore consider how the school might build a culture which facilitates the appropriate balance.

Building the school culture

As Peters and Waterman (*op. cit.*) observe, those in the school charged with building a culture which encourages excellence could do worse than look at the classroom.

> Studies in the classroom, for example, suggest that effective classes are the ones in which discipline is sure: students are expected to come to class on time; homework is regularly turned in and graded. On the other hand, those same classrooms as a general rule emphasize positive feedback, posting good reports, praise and coaching by the teacher.

In this context the 'rules' are seen as crucial; dealing with 'quality, service, innovation and experimentation,' their focus is on growing and developing the individual's thinking and work contributions to the organisation. This is achieved by creating a culture in which, secure about their shared values and objectives, individuals bring their own creativity to bear on organisational challenges and problems.

It is our assumption that problems and problem-solving are a central part of the processes of education. Schools should be places where teachers and pupils are engaged in activities that help them to become more successful in understanding and dealing with the problems they meet. In this sense problems that occur in schools, and important decisions that have to be made, can be seen as opportunities for learning. Ideally, therefore, schools should be organised in ways that encourage all those involved, pupils and teachers, to work cooperatively in order to learn through problem-solving.

Unfortunately, too often schools seem to be organised in ways that inhibit cooperation and problem-solving. For example, Gitlin (1987) has investigated the impact of organisational and curriculum structures on the work of teachers and pupils. His view is that 'common school structures encourage a teacher that emphasises management and technical skills, isolate teachers from one another, and "disconnect" them from their students'. Skrtic (1988) characterises schools as professional bureaucracies that are unsuited to the stimulation of divergent thinking patterns. Rather, such organisations tend to use what Mintzberg (1979) has called 'pigeon-holing', a process by which problems that occur are matched to one of a series of existing responses. Mintzberg suggests that a common difficulty associated with the idea of pigeon-holing is that 'the professional confuses the needs of his clients with the skills he has to offer them'.

If we are to find ways of encouraging collaborative problem-solving and Collaborative School Management in order to bring about policy improvements, we have to be sensitive to the nature of schools as organisations. Most of all we have to remind ourselves that schools are more than a collection of buildings, timetables and curricular plans. First and foremost they are about relationships and interactions between people. Consequently a successful school is likely to be one in which relationships and interactions are facilitated and coordinated in order that those involved feel that they are enaged in a common mission. Commenting on effective schools and school change, Skrtic (*op. cit.*) argues that 'at bottom, the difference is people. People acting on their values and affecting what the organisation can be'. Or, as Clark *et al.* (1984) suggest, 'The search for excellence in schools is the search for excellence in people'.

Why, then, is this idea of people working collaboratively to solve problems and achieve common purposes so difficult to achieve in schools? One difficulty is that the 'loose-coupling' within schools comes about not because there are shared values and objectives but because they consist of units, processes, actions and individuals that tend to operate in isolation from one another. Such fragmentation is further encouraged by the goal ambiguity that is a feature of schooling. Despite the rhetoric of curriculum aims and objectives schools consist of people who have very different values and, indeed, beliefs about the purposes of education. To illustrate this point Weick uses the metaphor of a soccer game in which players enter and leave the game at will, and attempt to kick the ball towards several goals that are scattered haphazardly around a circular pitch.

Johnson and Johnson (1989) suggest that schools can be structured in one of three ways: individualistically, competitively or cooperatively. In schools that have an individualistic form of organisation teachers work alone to achieve goals unrelated to the goals of their colleagues. Consequently there is no sense of common purpose, little sharing of expertise and limited support for individuals. Furthermore such schools often move towards what becomes in practice a more competitive form of organisation.

In a competitive context teachers strive to do better than their colleagues, recognising that their fate is negatively linked. In other words the career progress of one teacher is likely to be enhanced by the failure of others within their school. In this win-lose struggle to succeed it becomes almost inevitable that individuals celebrate the difficulties experienced by their colleagues, since these are likely to increase their own chances of success.

Clearly the organisational approach that is most likely to facilitate school development is one that emphasises and encourages cooperation. The aim must be to create, a more 'tightly-coupled' system without losing 'loose-coupling' benefits. In such a school staff strive for mutual benefit, recognising that they share a common fate. Individuals recognise, therefore, that their own success can be influenced positively by the performance of those around them. This being the case, individuals feel proud when a colleague succeeds and is recognised for professional competence. As Johnson and Johnson argue, 'A clear cooperative structure is the first prerequisite of an effective school'.

A school that achieves a cooperative organisational structure is likely to make good use of the expertise of all its personnel, provide a source of enrichment that will help foster their professional development, and encourage positive attitudes to the introduction of new ways of working. In short it provides the *context necessary for planning and implementing* school improvements.

At this point in the discussion it is important to stop and note that despite the case that has been made for greater cooperation within schools there is increasingly pressure on schools to move in a different direction. Competition between schools and within schools is currently seen by some as a means of improving educational standards (e.g. Sexton, 1988). This rationale is based on a view of education as the means of enhancing life chances, status and employment in the adult world (Hartnett and Naish, 1990). Furthermore schools are seen as input–output mechanisms, in which the pupils are working units who should go on to serve the technology of society, via its economic structures. In such a view of schooling, Bottery (1988) argues, children 'are merely means to an end, just as the teachers in an organisation are as well. The children are the future parts for an industrial machine, the teachers are their shapers and oilers'.

Clearly, our own picture of the self-managing school is based upon a very different view of the purposes of schooling. This is why we continue to emphasise the distinction between efficiency and effectiveness in educational context. It is also why we see the need to encourage teacher participation in goal-setting, reviewing, planning and implementation. Management is not antithetical to, but a major determinant of, educational quality. Therefore we must try to involve as many staff as possible actively in the management process of the school. To achieve participation in planning what is to happen there will need to be dialogue about the outcomes of any review between members of staff. At this stage, therefore, it is important to consider how staff can be practically involved in planning activities which are *effective*. One possible strategy is to use planning meetings.

A planning meeting can be regarded as being effective when:

- the knowledge and resources of all participants are used;
- time is well spent;
- it leads to high-quality conclusions;
- group members feel committed to any decisions that are made;
- the ability of members to work as a group is enhanced.

Keeping these criteria in mind it can be helpful to use more structured group processes as a means of encouraging participation. Such approaches may be used with groups of staff, pupils or indeed parents. Their strength is that when they are used well they can provide a secure context in which individuals feel able to make meaningful contributions within meetings, rather than simply 'attend' them. The most common approaches are considered below.

(i) *Brainstorming*

This approach is valuable in creating an agenda for discussion. It involves a set period when participants suggest points or comments relating to the area under discussion. One member of the group records these contributions, preferably on a blackboard or overhead projector. Strict rules are kept during the brainstorming in order that participants feel confident to make their suggestions without fear of criticism. Essential rules are as follows:

- All ideas related to the issue in any direct way are desired.
- A maximum number of related ideas is desired.
- One idea may be modified, adapted and expressed as another idea.
- Ideas should be expressed as clearly and concisely as possible.
- No discussion of the ideas should be attempted.
- No criticism of ideas is accepted.

Once the brainstorming period is over, the list of points generated provides an agenda for normal discussion.

(ii) *Twos and fours*

This is a very useful approach for encouraging individuals to discuss their own positions on an issue. It is also generally a good way of encouraging discussion. First of all the group discuss the issues in pairs for a time. Then two pairs join up to compare notes and to try to come to some joint agreement about their position. Finally, the various groups join together for discussion. The advantage of this approach is that the views of all individuals are expressed at some stage.

(iii) *Stance-taking*

In this approach two groups prepare opposite sides of an argument about a matter of concern (e.g. integration of children with disabilities). Pairs are then formed of individuals from each group. They then present their arguments to one another. Through this process individuals can gain a deeper understanding of the complexities of the issue.

(iv) *Structured problem-solving*

This approach is particularly advantageous when reviewing what has been achieved with a view to deciding what are the problems and how these can best be overcome. The steps involved are as follows:

(1) Groups of three are set up. One of the participants takes on the role of 'explainer' and the other two act as 'clarifiers'. The 'explainer' explains what they have done and the problems they have encountered. It is then the job of the 'clarifiers' to ensure that what is being said is fully understood by all. They should not pass value-judgements.

(2) The role of 'explainer' rotates so that all three get a chance to discuss what they have been doing.

(3)   After each person has discussed what they have been doing, an agreed list of difficulties facing each one is drawn up. Each difficulty is then itemised on a separate card.

(4)   The sets of cards are passed to another member of the group, who reviews the difficulty stated on the card, and then on the reverse tries to complete the sentence 'Have you considered...'

(5)   This process is repeated with another member of the group.

(6)   The responses are reviewed by the whole group.

(v)   *Nominal group technique*

This is a more sophisticated strategy for structuring group discussion. Its strengths are that it:

● ensures that all participants contribute;
● avoids the dominance of a few people who have particularly strong views;
● encourages a flexible interpretation of the issue under consideration;
● ensures a wide range of responses;
● allows a systematic ordering of priorities.

The technique requires a group leader, who must remain neutral throughout the activity. The procedure is carried out as follows:

(1)   **Clarification of the task:** The task is presented on a blackboard or overhead projector (e.g. What aspects of the curriculum do we need to reconsider?). In order that all participants fully understand the question, time is spent in group discussion about the nature of the task.

(2)   **Silent nominations:** Individuals are given a fixed period to list their own private responses. This should not be hurried. They are then asked to rank their own list in order to establish felt priorities.

(3)   **Master list:** The group leader compiles a master list on the blackboard or overhead projector taking one item from each group member in rotation. No editing of the material is allowed and no evaluative comments are to be made at this stage. It is helpful to number the items.

(4)   **Item classification:** During this phase each item is discussed until all members know what it means. Clarification only is allowed. If a member of the group now feels that their item is already covered by someone else's, they may request its withdrawal. No pressure

should be applied to any individual to have items withdrawn or incorporated in another.

(5) **Evaluation:** It is now necessary to decide the relative importance of items in the eyes of the group. Each person is allowed five weighted votes (i.e. five points for the item that is felt to be most important, four points for the next, and so on). A simple voting procedure allows the consensus to emerge.

Once the composite picture has emerged, it provides an agenda for normal group discussions to proceed.

(vi) *Brickwalls*

This approach can be particularly valuable when considering the implementation of a plan. The aim is to help participants define their future priorities and deal with possible obstacles. Individuals are asked to draw a mountain. At the top of the mountain they write down their objective (e.g. To improve my use of cooperative learning in my classroom). They then sketch a brickwall in front of their mountain. Each brick in the wall represents a possible obstacle that may prevent the individual from reaching his/her goal. 'Obstacles' are written onto the bricks. In small groups there is discussion in order to consider how the bricks in the wall might be moved out of the way. Participants may also be asked to consider how far the obstacles are of their own making.

(vii) *Reviewing previous meetings*

One final point worth making about the development of more effective group meetings is that it helps to talk openly about how meetings are going. Allowing a few minutes to discuss the effectiveness of how a meeting or series of meetings has been conducted focuses the minds of all involved on the issues of how they can be made more beneficial. It may also be that such discussions throw up suggestions for their improvement.

Summary

This chapter has looked at a number of possible approaches to planning. In so doing, we acknowledge that there is much that can be learned from corporate planning systems, but express some reservation about the extent to which 'techniques' can become activities in their own right, separated from the real purposes and activities of the school. We therefore recommend that planning mechanisms are kept simple and are not 'mystified' by a special jargon or by becoming the preserve of a small staff group. The view put forward by Peters and Waterman is advocated as particularly helpful here.

It is then suggested that plans will be required to cover a number of areas of school life. A model showing how such plans can be coordinated is put forward, together with possible criteria which could be used to assess the quality of planning activity in these areas. Finally the issue of how the school might develop a culture which encourages staff to play a full and appropriate role in the planning cycle was considered, and we make some suggestions about developing school climate.

These approaches are offered simply as examples of how one aspect of the school's culture, the meetings it holds to discuss planning issues, could be managed in a way which encourages participation and supports individual growth. There are many aspects of the school's culture where similar attention as to how, *specifically*, the climate can be enhanced can lead to the development of the 'loose–tight' properties which promote high quality debate without damaging personal relationships.

CHAPTER SIX

From Planning to Action

Plans in themselves have no particular value unless they lead to some form of action. Indeed the existence of plans that have been produced by considerable effort and yet have not been implemented can be demoralising to staff. This kind of 'rhetoric-reality' gap with respect to attempted innovation is quite common in schools and it can have the effect of undermining staff confidence and commitment.

Our aim is to increase confidence and, in so doing, bring about improvements in practice that will make the school more effective. In this chapter, therefore, we focus attention on issues related to the successful implementation of development plans (see Figure 6.1).

An examination of the research findings about effective schools and successful teaching (e.g. Bickel and Bickel, 1986; Brophy, 1983; Mortimore *et al.*, 1988; Rosenshine, 1983; Rutter *et al.*, 1979) might seem to suggest that improving schools is relatively straightforward.

Figure 6.1   The efficiency cycle

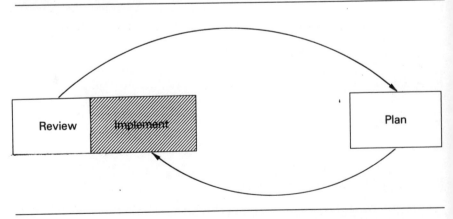

Presumably if we know what good schools and effective teaching look like, we have a recipe for bringing about improvements.

Alas, applying the lessons from the research is not so simple. Schools and classrooms are complex environments, involving a range of unpredictable and interacting factors. They are also subject to many external constraints and influences. Consequently bringing about improvements can be a difficult and, at times, frustrating business. Change, particularly when it involves new ways of thinking and behaving, is difficult and time-consuming to bring about. Fullan (1982) argues that for it to be achieved successfully, change has to be understood and accepted by those involved. Understanding and acceptance take time and need encouragement. These problems are made even more complex when they occur in schools by what Iano (1986) refers to as the 'inarticulate component of practice' – in other words, the difficult to articulate practical knowledge that is acquired only through practice and contact with other practitioners.

In considering how plans for school development can be implemented successfully, therefore, it is important to take account of what is known about change in educational settings (e.g. see Fullan, 1982; Huberman and Miles, 1984).

Understanding change

In order to better understand the nature of change it is helpful to reflect on personal experience. Think about some attempt to introduce a new way of working into your own school or classroom. How did it go? Did it work? How long did it take? Were there some aspects that were more successful than others? How did people react?

As we reflect on our own experiences of attempts to introduce new ideas or ways of working into schools (keeping in mind the research evidence that is available) a number of thoughts come to mind:

- change is really about learning
- change is a process, not an event
- change takes time
- change can be confusing
- change can hurt.

Let us consider these points in some detail:

(i) *Change is really about learning*

Change is essentially about learning new ways of thinking and behaving.

If we accept this, it opens up a very helpful avenue of enquiry. It suggests that in seeking to understand how to handle change, alone or with colleagues, we can get some useful ideas from considering what we already know about learning. What are the circumstances that help people learn? Whatever these are (and we will be considering them in some detail later) they are likely to be helpful in schools when teachers are attempting to improve their own practice.

Accepting that change is really about learning has a further significant implication. It means that schools should be places where teachers learn from experience in the same way as they intend that their pupils should learn from the tasks and activities in which they are engaged. Indeed, we would go further and suggest that teachers who regard *themselves* as learners in the classroom are likely to be more successful in facilitating the learning of their pupils.The sensitivity they acquire as a result of reflecting upon their own attempts to learn new ideas or new ways of working is influencial in terms of the way they deal with the children in their classes.

(ii) *Change is a process, not an event*

If we are talking about the introduction of significant changes, involving the adoption of new ways of thinking and different ways of operating in the classroom, it is important to recognise that this is usually a process of adjustment rather than an event in time. Fundamental ideas do not change in a moment, nor are new approaches implemented in the blinking of an eye. What happens is that a sequence of changes or operations is undergone as the individual adjusts to the new circumstances or requirements.

Once again, it can be helpful to reflect upon personal experience of attempted innovation. No doubt particular events can be recalled; perhaps an introductory meeting to discuss what was to happen; or the first attempt to use some new materials in class. In order to fully understand the nature of the new approach and to become proficient in its use, however, it is usually necessary to go through a period of trial and error, possible confusion, difficulty and occasional elation. Gradually, if the change is successful, the process leads to feelings of greater confidence and personal development. In time, the practice and its principles eventually become personalised, i.e. linked to, and integrated with, existing aspects of thinking and practice.

(iii) *Change takes time*

Accepting that significant changes in teaching occur as a process takes us on to the next point. Because it is a process, changes takes place over time.

Consequently, in attempting to handle change successfully we need to be aware of the importance of time, particularly in terms of:

- the need for time to be available to learn about new ideas and to practise new skills;
- the need to recognise that the process of 'personalising' new ways of working will take time.

Too often in schools teachers are expected to make changes overnight. 'As from Monday we will start using the new maths scheme' or 'In September, classes will be mixed ability'. The pressure of unrealistic time-scales can create stress, anxiety and negative reactions to what is proposed. It can also mean that little or no opportunity exists to learn more about *how to implement* the proposed changes.

Evidence from social psychology suggests that complex organisations, such as schools, can take from three to five years to fully adopt a new way of working. Yet so often in education the time-scale set for a major innovation in practice is much shorter. Recently, this has been further complicated by requiring teachers to deal with a number of new initiatives at the same time, thus diffusing energy and effort.

(iv) *Change can be confusing*

Textbooks about management in schools sometimes give the impression that change is a rational process, a series of activities to be followed like so many boxes in a flowchart. Establish what you want to do, how you are going to do it, and so on, then just pitch in. What we must not lose sight of, however, is that the time-consuming process of learning that we call change is, in practice, often confusing. As individuals seek to relate new ideas and ways of working to their own unique range of personal experiences, preferences and prejudices, these can become distorted, adapted or, indeed, totally subverted into a form that is more acceptable. Consequently the original purpose, despite having been presented in a logical and rational form, may come to mean something quite different as a result of its adoption by other people.

This does not mean that frameworks are not useful, but that we should be aware of the limitations of 'rational' models.

(v) *Change can hurt*

The final point we wish to make in our account of the nature of change in schools is to do with its effect on people. Human beings in general prefer to stay as they are. Making changes requires risk-taking, it is so much safer to stay as you are. Also if you adopt something new then you often have to reject something else, and this can be painful. Asking people to alter their ideas, possibly requiring them to reject aspects of their past practice, has the potential to cause considerable damage.

Barriers to change

What, then, are the things that can get in the way as teachers attempt to learn new ideas and introduce new ways of working? Our experience suggests that a number of factors that can be barriers to change commonly arise. These are:

- lack of understanding
- lack of necessary skills
- existing attitudes
- limited resources
- inappropriate organisation

We will consider each of these factors in turn.

(i) *Lack of understanding*

In order to adopt a new way of working it is necessary to have a reasonable understanding of what it involves, what is the purpose and how will it effect the people involved. Without such an understanding, commitment is likely to be limited and attempts are going to be at best tentative and, more frequently, flawed. Teachers have a capacity to pretend that they are doing something when, in fact, they are not. Furthermore, it takes a certain amount of professional courage to admit in front of your colleagues that you don't really understand. So, for example, the deputy head explains a proposal at a staff meeting. 'This is what I am suggesting, this is why, and so on. Does everybody understand? Is everybody clear?' At this point some teachers may find it difficult to express their concerns or explain their lack of understanding. As a result the initiative proceeds with some colleagues, at least, far from clear about what it really entails.

Those in a school who are leading or coordinating developments may, as a result of their own enthusiasm, inadvertently make this problem of lack of understanding worse. If they have spent a lot of time thinking about, planning and trying out a new idea themselves and wish to share it with their colleagues, they may impose a schedule that allows little opportunity for understanding to occur. Their enthusiasm and commitment may lead them to be insensitive to the needs of their colleagues as learners.

(ii) *Lack of necessary skills*

It may be, of course, that the need for change is understood but people feel that they do not have the competence to carry it out. Indeed, their feelings may be correct – they may not have the necessary skills.

Once again, the enthusiasm and commitment of others can cause difficulties and possible stress. It can be very uncomfortable for an individual to feel that some of their colleagues are able to do things that they know are currently beyond their own competence. This discomfort will be made worse if, in their desire to get on, certain colleagues commit themselves (and others) to a time scale for implementation that allows no opportunity for individuals to develop their skills.

This is a particular problem in schools where there is no tradition of talking about techniques and approaches and no facility for teachers to work collaboratively as they attempt to introduce new ways of working. Regrettably, it is the case that many teachers go through their careers without having opportunities to observe how others organise things in their classrooms. Their models of teaching have evolved from their own experience as pupils at school and as a result of their own trial-and-error efforts over the years. Whilst we would not wish to underestimate the value of learning by trial and error, we also know how much can be learned by watching others teaching and working collaboratively alongside colleagues.

(iii) *Existing attitudes*

We also have to recognise that sometimes the most significant barriers to improvement are those that are erected in our own minds. Sometimes, in our own work, we invite teachers to identify those factors which appear to be interfering with progress towards their professional goals. Often they produce extensive lists of reasons outside of themselves, particularly reasons that relate to the attitudes and behaviour of their colleagues. We press them to consider what obstacles they create as a result of their own attitudes and behaviour and this quite often leads people to recognise that there are a number of 'blockages' that they could, themselves, remove.

Having said that, it is clear that education takes place within a complex social environment and that other people do intrude as we attempt to develop our work as teachers. A common mistake in this respect is to personalise difficulties, suggesting that some individual or group of individuals constitutes resistance and is preventing change. Our experience suggests that this view, though common, is unhelpful. Once an individual is seen as 'the problem' it becomes very difficult to enrol their support and involvement. It is likely that attitudes towards them will become apparent, perhaps through use of language or mode of expression towards them. As a result, their negative view of what is proposed will become reinforced and the chances of change of mind become even less.

It is healthier to view colleagues who are currently resisting what is being proposed as serving an appropriate professional role, in examining and questioning its value. Indeed, given that education has been somewhat prone to 'bandwagon' ideas of late, it is important that all teachers show some willingness to resist. This being the case, the colleague who is expressing reservations can be seen as helping others to understand and evaluate what is proposed. This also has the added tactical advantage that everybody involved, including those who are sceptical, retains the right to adjust their views; this is particularly important since there are few absolute truths in education.

(iv) *Limited resources*

At a more practical level, attempts to innovate can easily be frustrated if the necessary resources are unavailable. This can take a variety of forms.

It may, for example, be that the introduction of some new scheme is inhibited because there are not enough copies of the materials available. If teachers have continually to send children searching around the school for the resources box or set of books, they may eventually come to the view that it is easier to use something else.

A lack of resources may also relate to the human resources available. As we have seen, change often requires time to try out new ideas and to discuss their use with colleagues. When a teacher has a full timetable this may become something of a deterrent.

(v) *Inappropriate organisation*

Related to the use of resources is the issue of organisation. Sometimes when a proposal gets into difficulty it is because the overall organisation of the school, or the organisational pattern within particular classes, prevents the new way of working from being implemented.

For example, the staff in one primary school wanted to try the idea of an integrated day as a means of increasing flexibility within classes and meeting children's individual needs. The idea was that children should have greater choice over the activities in which they took part and that pupils would be involved in a variety of different activities in various parts of the room. The organisation problem was that several teachers were absolutely committed to the idea that each child should have his or her own seat. They felt that 'having a place' in the classroom was a source of security for the child. Unfortunately, this meant that there was a need for thirty or so chairs. Chairs and table spaces in these classrooms then militated against the idea of a more flexible form of organisation.

The list of possible barriers to change, though by no means comprehensive, is potentially rather depressing. Thinking about it can leave teachers wondering if change is actually possible, given the complexities and pressures of day-to-day life in schools. Yet clearly it is possible, particularly as each of these barriers can be avoided. Indeed, recognising their existence is the first stage in a strategy for avoiding them.

Checking readiness

It makes sense in planning the implementation of new approaches or methods to consider the 'readiness' of a school for what is involved (Hubermann and Miles, 1984). As a result of extensive research in Canada, Fullan and Park (1981) have drawn attention to a range of contextual factors that are likely to have a bearing upon the success or failure of attempts at innovation. Their concern is focused particularly on the 'implementation' phase. They define this as 'The process of altering existing practice in order to achieve more effectively certain desired learning outcomes for pupils'.

Their research suggests that twelve interacting factors seem to influence implementation (see Figure 6.2). We have developed a schedule based on this evidence that has proved helpful to groups of teachers in planning the implementation of developments in their own schools (see Figure 6.3). It provides an agenda that can be used to assess positive and negative factors in a particular context.

Figure 6.2   Twelve factors influencing implementation

CHARACTERISTICS OF THE INNOVATION OR REVISION
(1)   Need for the change
(2)   Clarity, complexity of the change
(3)   Quality and availability of materials

CHARACTERISTICS AT THE SCHOOL SYSTEM LEVEL
(4)   History of innovative attempts
(5)   Expectations and training for principals
(6)   Teacher input and professional development (in-service, technical assistance)
(7)   Board and community support
(8)   Time-line and monitoring
(9)   Overload

CHARACTERISTICS AT THE SCHOOL LEVEL
(10) Principals' actions
(11) Teacher/teacher relations and actions

FACTORS EXTERNAL TO THE SCHOOL SYSTEM
(12) Role of the Ministry of Education and other educational agencies.

Whilst the schedule should not be seen as 'rocket science', it does provide a useful basis for discussion. Broadly speaking, the more positive responses there are to the 12 questions, the greater the chance of successful implementation. In addition it encourages those involved to consider *what actions* might be taken to create a more positive culture for change.

Developing a culture for change

In this section we consider some general factors that seem to be helpful to teachers as they attempt to develop their practice and adopt new ways of working. Together they are factors that lead to a culture that is conducive to change. They are:

● clarity of purpose
● realistic goals
● motivation
● support
● resources
● evaluation

We will consider each of these factors in turn.

(i) *Clarity of purpose*

As we have seen, an understanding of what is intended by a proposed change is essential to its successful implementation. It is important to note that a proposal can mean different things to different people. Reality is something that each of us constructs in our minds as a result of our previous experience. Consequently when we talk about finding ways of helping colleagues to understand the purpose and nature of what is intended we must accept that this may change as a result of the process of discussion and collaboration. The important feature is that time should

Figure 6.3   Implementing change in school

IMPLEMENTATION   'The process of altering existing practice in order to achieve more effectively certain desired outcomes for pupils.'

According to Fullan and Park (1981) twelve factors seem to be especially critical. Consider these with respect to your own development plans.

	Yes	No	Not sure
A. The nature of the change 1 Do those involved accept the need for change? 2 Is the proposed change understood by those involved? 3 Are necessary resources available?			
B. Characteristics of the school system 4 Have previous attempts at change been successful? 5 Do the Headteacher and others who will need to take a lead have support? 6 Will there be staff development for all those involved? 7 Is the change supported by the Governors and parents? 8 Are there plans to monitor the process of implementation over time? 9 Are there strategies to avoid overload as a result of too many innovations during the same period?			
C. Characteristics of the school 10 Is the Headteacher prepared to take an active role in supporting the change? 11 Will teachers provide support for one another?			
D. External factors 12 Will there be support from external agencies?			

be found to allow individuals to gain a sense of personal meaning about what is to happen, in order that they can become comfortable with, and committed to, what is proposed.

(ii) *Realistic goals*

Given the existence of an agreed purpose, the next stage must be to formulate some plan to make it happen. Once again, time becomes a critical issue and it is important that realistic priorities are set, taking into account other demands and the need to allow people space and opportunity to learn new skills that may be necessary in order to implement what is being proposed. It makes sense, therefore, to set goals – for example, 'This is what we will try to achieve by the summer'. These provide a common sense of purpose and should encourage participation, particularly if the goals seem to be achievable to those involved.

(iii) *Motivation*

In order to encourage involvement and effort there has to be a desire to change that is the result of either internal or external pressures. Pressure can take many forms, and if it is inappropriate or excessive may have a negative effect on attitudes. Often the most beneficial type of pressure arises from the desire of individuals to improve their own professional competence (i.e. personal pressure) or from participation in some form of cooperative venture (i.e. peer pressure).

(iv) *Support*

It also helps to have a strong sense of support. Making changes in the way you teach requires you to take risks with your professional credibility. All the evidence suggests that most of us are more likely to take risks if we are with others who provide encouragement and help. At the implementation stage, in particular, it is helpful to have the advice and comments of respected and trusted colleagues. There is, therefore, a need to create an atmosphere of support within a school that encourages individual members of staff to try new ways of working.

It is important to note here that support is important for *all* staff, including headteachers and others who have management roles.

(v) *Resources*

A vital management task is to ensure that the resources necessary for the introduction of what is proposed are available. Whether at a personal level or at a whole school level, it means establishing priorities and then seeing to it that decisions about the use of time, human energy and the allocation of materials are made in order to enable these priorities to be achieved.

(vi) *Evaluation*

Finally it is important that the introduction of any new way of working is carefully monitored. In particular we need to know:

- Are we getting anywhere?
- Could things be improved? If so, how?
- How do the people involved feel?

In this sense, evaluation is not a set of scientific principles and complex procedures but simply an attitude of mind. It is about setting aside time (yes, more time) to reflect on what is happening, in order to make changes as necessary. It seems so straightforward when expressed in this common-sense way but, frankly, it is something that is often overlooked. In their enthusiasm to bring about improvements, headteachers in particular can set off towards their goals, allowing no opportunity for what is happening to be examined and improved in the light of experience. For those seeking more help in this area, Hopkins (1989) provides an excellent source of evaluation techniques.

Getting started

In their booklet on School Development Plans, Hargreaves *et al.* (1989) suggest a series of steps for making such a plan work. They suggest that this involves:

- sustaining commitment during implementation;
- checking the progress of implementation;
- overcoming any problems encountered;
- checking the success of implementation;
- taking stock;
- reporting progress.

They also outline some practical ideas with respect to each of these steps, and, in particular, their comments on the linking of objectives to tasks, and on establishing evaluation procedures ('success checks') are both direct and helpful.

Building from this, in this concluding section we outline two specific strategies that we have found valuable in drawing together the information and processes required for successful implementation.

Using force field analysis

The first strategy is based upon the ideas of Kurt Lewin (1951) and is known as *force field analysis*. It provides a means of analysing organisational structures in order to find ways of dealing with them constructively. Such situations are assumed to be subject to two opposing sets of forces. Everard and Morris (1985) suggest that these forces might be 'needs, drives, aspirations, fears and other feelings generated either within oneself or in interpersonal, inter-group or organisational-environmental situations affected by a proposed change . . . ' On the one hand some of these may be seen as 'driving forces', likely to help facilitate the proposal; on the other hand there may be 'restraining forces' that seek to limit such movement. Force field analysis is concerned with the identification of these forces, their direction and their strength.

The aim must be, therefore, to remove or weaken the restraining forces in order to encourage the desired change. Another possibility is to intensify the driving forces, but experience suggests that if this is done without a concomitant decrease in restraining forces it can lead to counter-productive tensions within an organisation.

Everard and Morris (1985) recommend that the approach be used as a basis for group problem solving, using the following steps:

(1) Define specifically the change that is desired, and ensure mutual understanding.

(2) Consider all the forces at work in the present situation; do not consider possible or hoped-for events or solutions. Try to understand the forces felt by the people or groups affected by the change – not by the group doing the analysis.

(3) On a simple diagram (so that the situation can be readily visualised), draw arrows proportional in length to the strength of the forces, and label them. If insufficient information is available to estimate the strength, decide how it can be obtained.

Figure 6.4   Using force field analysis

Stage 1 – Defining the desired change

The present situation

The situation we hope to achieve

Stage 2 – Analysing the forces

INHIBITING FORCES

What is making it difficult to implement the desired change?

1.

2.

3.

4.

5.

6.

FACILITATING FORCES

What can be tapped into/drawn on to help bring about the desired change?

1.

2.

3.

4.

5.

6.

Stage 3 – Considering the field

INHIBITING FORCES	Possible actions to reduce or eliminate these
FACILITATING FORCES	Possible actions to increase these

106

Stage 4 – Agreeing an action plan

ACTION PLAN			
What needs doing?	Who will be responsible?	What resources will be needed?	When will it be carried out?

Figure6.4 provides a four-stage format for groups of teachers wishing to try this approach in order to plan for a particular change. The stages are as follows:

Stage 1 Defining the desired change
With respect to a particular area of development the present situation and desired situation are described as accurately as possible.

Stage 2 Analysing the forces
Those involved in the development identify those forces that seem to be operating on the situation which can either facilitate or inhibit the changes desired.

Stage 3 Considering the field
The forces identified are considered in terms of their relative strength. This provides an agenda for considering problems and strategies that might be adopted, e.g. should attention be concentrated on removing or reducing obstacles, or on building up strengths?

Stage 4 Agreeing an action plan
Having considered the various forces at work and what actions might be taken, this analysis is now coordinated into a specific action plan.

Learning need analysis

The second strategy to facilitate implementation is based upon the work of Hersey and Blanchard (1972). They refer to four interrelated types of change involving:

● knowledge
● attitudes
● individual behaviour
● group behaviour

They see these four elements as being incremental in terms of how they influence one another, and hierarchical with respect to how much learning they require. So, for example, changes in attitude tend to precede changes in individual behaviour, whilst changes in individual behaviour are more difficult to achieve than changes to attitude.

Developing this approach, Figure 6.5 suggests a format that can be used to plan for change. It involves the following three steps:

Figure 6.5 Planning for change – learning need analysis

1. Identify the particular change which you plan to implement. Briefly list its objectives.

2. How will you recognise whether the change has been successful? List any criteria or measures you can use to indicate success.

3. Think about the people who will be carrying through/affected by the change. Think in particular about what they need to know, what they need to feel, and what they need to be able to do if this change is to be successful. List these:

(i) They will need to develop knowledge/understanding of:

(ii) They will need to develop positive attitudes towards/about:

(iii) They will need to develop the skill necessary to be able to:

4. Taking the lists of knowledge, attitudes and skills identified, place these in rank order according to how influential you believe each will be in successfully implementing the change. Then consider how to bring each development about; what action is required? By whom? What resources will be involved?

Development need	Required action	Person responsible	Resources required

(1) Agreement about the nature of the change that is desired.
(2) A classification of the learning needs the change generates for those individuals involved.
(3) A format for prioritising and planning strategies for supporting individuals as they attempt to develop the knowledge, skills and attitudes necessary for implementing the change.

The 'learning need' approach is particularly valuable in determining the staff development needs that will be necessary to facilitate a particular innovation. As we have noted above, an appropriate staff development programme can be a powerful means of supporting the implementation of new ways of working.

Summary

This concluding chapter has considered the problem of translating plans into action. It has suggested that precipitating action requires an understanding of how change affects individuals and organisations, and has identified some of the barriers and problems to be overcome. Factors that can inhibit change are noted and recommendations made as to how conditions for successful implementation can be created.

Finally, drawing on our own experience of working with teachers, we suggest some ways of planning for/engaging with specific developments in schools which we have found helpful. Such approaches tend to integrate planning for curricular (or other organisational) objectives with specific plans to develop staff and other resources needed if implementation is to be successful and sustained.

Postscript

While we have been writing this book during the hot, English summer of 1990 our belief in its relevance has been continually reinforced by the contents of the national press. Almost every day there has been coverage of developments that seem to complicate further the context within which schools have to be managed.

Amongst recent announcements have been indications that a number of policies that emanated from the 1988 Education Act are likely to be modified. For example, reports from the field-testing of assessment materials related to Key Stage 1 suggest that these have proved to be impractical. We must assume, therefore, that these will be significantly altered before they are fully implemented. Consequently schools are being asked to prepare for the use of these approaches without any real idea of the form they will take.

There have also been reports that the extent of and time scale for the implementation of the requirements of Key Stages 1 and 2 of the National Curriculum may be modified. Recent government comment upon the much awaited report on Art, Music and Physical Education suggests that the requirements for teaching these subjects to pupils in the 14+ age group may be changed. In addition confusion still continues as to the likely relationship between Key Stage 4 and the GCSE examination.

Finally, to add to the general air of uncertainty, there has been much speculation about a possible move away from central pay bargaining with respect to teachers' salaries.

Given all these developments it seems to us that those charged with the running of schools must act with sensitivity and authority in order to protect the morale and welfare of their colleagues. More specifically they should, as we have argued throughout this book, encourage teachers to recognise and stand by their core educational values. They should also take responsibility for helping their colleagues to collaborate in reviewing policies, planning developments and implementing plans for improvement. Success in these management tasks will not only determine the quality of education we offer our children, it will also reduce the enormous stress currently placed upon teachers.

APPENDIX ONE

Using an audit matrix

The employment of simple matrices within the review process is not new, but the requirements placed upon schools to deliver specified curricular patterns has greatly increased both the relevance and use made of this approach. We have suggested (see Chapter Four) that schools will find the audit matrix a versatile review technique and that it offers a relatively quick and cost-effective method of both compiling and displaying information. Indeed, the advantages of the visual summary it offers can be a significant factor in communicating with staff.

Of course, the reliability and validity of information gathered this way will be determined by the *way the process is carried out*. Key issues related to how the matrix is used centre on such questions as focus, timing, and the numbers and levels of staff who contribute information. Thus, for example, if we look at how 'auditing' has been applied in some schools following promptings from the National Curriculum Council, we will see that it can be both divisive and counterproductive to focus too narrowly on particular subject areas in the first instance. The following charts are offered not as exemplars, but simply to illustrate how a matrix can be used to bring together staff in analysing pupil learning experiences rather than divide them into 'subject' specialists defending their own curriculum space. The charts relate to *four stages* through which an audit could be conducted.

Chart One illustrates how a school might review its current curriculum pattern in light of the National Curriculum requirements. It is intended to be applied across a whole age cohort within the school, and commences the audit process by building up a picture of where particular curricular experiences are made available to pupils. It is suggested that at this initial stage:

114

CHART ONE National Curriculum audit 1 – Curriculum coverage

													PROGRAMMES OF STUDY	Year (1–11)
													English	CORE AND FOUNDATION SUBJECTS
													Maths	
													Science	
													History	
													Geography	
													Technology	
													Modern foreign language	
													Art	
													Music	
													Physical education	
													Religious education	
													Economic/ industrial awareness	CROSS CURRICULAR THEMES
													Careers education	
													Health education	
													Environmental education	
													Education for citizenship	
													Equal opportunities	CROSS CURRICULAR DIMENSIONS
													Multi-culturalism	

116

CHART TWO National Curriculum audit 2 – Skills and learning opportunities

												PROGRAMMES OF STUDY	Year (1–11)
												Communication	SKILLS
												Numeracy	
												Problem solving	
												Personal and social	
												Information technology	
												Study	
												Enquiry based	LEARNING OPPORTUNITIES
												Experiental-practical	
												Technology based	
												Group-centred	
												Individualised learning projects	
												Discussion centred	

CHART THREE National Curriculum audit 3 – Assessment mapping

Year (1–11)	KEYSTAGE:	SUBJECT:	COURSES/MODULES/ UNITS OF WORK							ATTAINMENT TARGETS

CHART FOUR National Curriculum audit 4 – Course/subject contribution matrix

							COURSES/MODULES/ UNITS OF WORK	COURSE/SUBJECT: KEYSTAGE:	Year (1–11)
									SUBJECT AND ATTAINMENT TARGETS
									CROSS CURRICULAR THEMES AND DIMENSIONS

(1) The *whole curriculum* offered to the particular year group is reviewed.

(2) *Teaching staff* working with that year group are invited to *contribute* (by completing the matrix for their own courses) to the overall picture.

(3) Teaching staff are encouraged to consider how, through the courses they offer, they contribute to *other subject content areas, and cross-curricular themes and dimensions.*

In a secondary school, this process could be co-ordinated by a Head of Year. In a primary or middle school some modification of the matrix may be necessary, but the same principle would apply – the idea is to get teachers to think about the match between organising categories into which they divide the curriculum for teaching purposes and the outcomes for pupils which the National Curriculum requires. At the end of this stage, the school would have a map of where the different experiences are offered and, in particular, where a number of courses contribute to one subject or cross curricular element.

Chart Two provides a vehicle for a similar analysis, but of *curriculum process* rather than content. The 'skills' pupils should have opportunities to develop are taken from the National Curriculum Council's recent publication *Curriculum Guidance 3 – The Whole Curriculum*. The 'learning opportunities' are simply offered as examples of the sort of processes a school might wish to monitor.

Again, we would recommend that the whole curriculum be audited, and that all teaching staff be invited to contribute information to the matrix.

Chart Three provides a format for mapping where in the curriculum pupils are prepared for particular attainment targets. If, for example, we were to take keystage 3 and English as points of focus, then we would be able to transfer from Chart One a list of *all those courses* which make a contribution to pupils' learning in this area. It is then possible to explore how the opportunities for developing English skills elsewhere in the curriculum helps to prepare the pupil for particular attainment targets. This activity would again be coordinated by the head of year, though several teachers may contribute.

Chart Four switches the emphasis away from how pupils are prepared for national assessments onto what overall contribution is to be made by any one subject grouping or course. In a secondary school, this chart would probably be completed by a department or faculty group, who would need to make sure they noted contributions the subject made to *other content areas and to cross-curricular elements* (see charts one, two and three), as well as checking the match between teaching programmes and assessment within the subject. In a primary school the exercise may be pulled together by the co-ordinator for a particular subject (e.g. maths, technology) and the courses listed may well be predominantly topic work or thematic in nature.

Such charts, once compiled, can provide a very important input into planning processes. They show at a glance where there are gaps and overlaps; they also remind teachers of their responsibilities to areas of the whole-curriculum which fall outside single subject boundaries.

We recognise that the detail of these particular charts may well not match the particular requirements of a given school, but hope readers will feel free to adapt and modify as necessary, so that the audit format they use suits the needs of the school, and its review processes.

APPENDIX TWO

Staffing audit

Another dimension of school life where an audit matrix can be useful is in analysing staff resources. As mentioned in Chapter Five, often schools have, at best, inadequate information about what individual teachers are able to offer. We have frequently met with headteachers who have spent considerable time and effort trying to find teachers with particular skills outside the school because they did not know they had teachers already inside the school with those same skills.

The two charts suggest how such information could be collated as a matter of routine (i.e. it can, once established, be updated each year with a minimum of time and effort). We suggest further that the charts be completed (in the smaller school by the headteacher or deputy, in the larger school by the person responsible for a particular curriculum or subject area) in consultation with individual members of staff.

Part One requires the person responsible for co-ordinating the completion to:

(1) Identify all the courses currently offered by the curriculum or subject team (or within the school in the case of a small primary) and list these in the section titled 'Teaching tasks'.

(2) List all staff who are, for the purposes of the audit, considered part of the teaching strength of that particular area (NB this would include headteachers and all those who contribute within the area).

(3) In consultation with the relevant member of staff, fill in the matrix. *Two* kinds of entry are desirable – first, the identification of current commitments; second, the identification of other courses the teacher could contribute to if required. It may be helpful to use a simple coding system here, for example, a square could be entered in the relevant box to show a current teaching activity, a circle to show that the teacher could offer or has offered an activity, though is not doing so currently.

Staffing Audit Part 1: Curriculum cover matrix

Personal details			CURRICULUM AREA/TEAM	Teaching tasks	Non-teaching tasks
AGE	SALARY GRADE	NO. TEACHING PERIODS	Name		

Staffing Audit Part 2: Individual development needs

Curriculum area	Name	Development opportunities	Selected priorities and methods	Person responsible for action

(4) It may be useful (though it is not essential) to collate basic personal details at the same time. The actual headings suggested are simply indicative: each school (or even curriculum group) could determine for itself what kind of biographical data is useful.

(5) Non-teaching tasks, such as the coordination of staff or other resources, the organisation of examinations or assessment processes, the responsibility for specialised equipment, can also be identified.

Once completed this matrix will allow two forms of analysis to be carried out.

● First, by reading down the columns it is possible to see the level of 'cover' or expertise available in relation to the courses offered. This can be particularly useful in helping to establish the organisation's staff development priorities, and in considering, for example, how a new course can be introduced, as it is possible to 'trace' the necessary changes through several courses and members of staff.

● Second, by reading along the rows of the matrix, individual needs/opportunities can be identified. These can be transferred to Part Two.

Part Two can then provide the basis of a staff development discussion, ideally with the individual teacher's line manager but possibly with a designated staff development coordinator. On this chart, the individual would identify those areas of the schools activity where he/she could develop appropriate skills. The discussion would then centre on which of these areas to follow up, and how. It would also seek to establish responsibility for following up at a level appropriate to the action required.

Clearly, where the school is using teacher appraisal, this could feed very useful information into the appraisal process.

References

Abbott, R. *et al.* (1988) *GRIDS Primary School Handbook*. Harlow: Longman.

Abbott, R. *et al.* (1988) *GRIDS Secondary School Handbook*. Harlow: Longman.

Abbott, R. *et al.* (1989) *External Perspectives on School Based Review*. York: Longman.

Acheson, K. A. and Gall, M. (1980) *Techniques in the Clinical Supervision of Teachers*. Harlow: Longman.

Adair, J. (1983) *Effective Leadership: a self-development manual*. Aldershot: Gower.

Ainscow, M. and Conner, C. (1990) *School-Based Inquiry*. Cambridge: Cambridge Institute of Education.

Anderson, L. W. and Burns, R. B. (1989) *Research in Classrooms*. Oxford: Pergamon.

Argyris, C. (1964) *Integrating the Individual and the Organization*. New York: Wiley.

Armitage, A. and Holden, P. (1989) *TVEI Staff Development; Manual 1*. Lancaster: Framework Press.

Becher, T. *et al.* (1981) *Policies for Educational Accountability*. London: Heinemann.

Bedfordshire Education Department (1990) *A Guide to Audits*. Bedford: Bedfordshire County Council.

Bell, J. (1987) *Doing Your Research Project*. Milton Keynes: Open University.

Bickel, W. E. and Bickel, D. D. (1986) 'Effective schools, classrooms and instruction: implications for special education'. *Exceptional Children*, **52** (6), 489–500.

Blake, R. R. and Mouton, J. S. (1964) *The Managerial Grid*. Houston: Gulf Publishing Company.

Bogdan, R. C. and Biklen, S. K. (1982) *Qualitative Data Analysis for Educational Research*. London: Croom Helm.

Bolam, R. (1984) 'Some practical generalisations about the change process' in Campbell, G. (ed) *Health Education and Youth: A Review of Research and Development*. London: Ward Lock Educational.

Bottery, M. P. (1988) 'Educational Management: an ethical critique'. *Oxford Review of Education* Vol 14, no 3, 341–351.

Bradley, H. W. *et al.* (1989) *Report on the Evaluation of the School Teacher Appraisal Pilot Study*. Cambridge: Cambridge Institute of Education.

Brophy, J. E. (1983) 'Classroom organisation and management'. *The Elementary School Journal*, **82**, 266–285.

Bush, T. (1986) *Theories of Educational Management*. London: Harper and Row.

Cabinet Office (1981) *Scrutiny of HM Inspectors of Schools in Scotland*. London: HMSO/Scottish Office.

Caldwell, B. J. and Spinks, J. M. (1988) *The Self-Managing School*. London: Falmer Press.

Campbell, D. T. Stanley, J. C. (1963) 'Experimental and quasi-experimental designs for research on teaching', in Gage, N. L. (ed) *Handbook of Research on Teaching*. Chicago: Rand McNally.

Carlson, D. (1967) *Modern Management*. Alhambra, CA: Tinnon-Brown.

Cave, E. and Wilkinson, C. (1990) *Local Management of Schools: some practical issues*. London: Routledge.

Clark, D. L., Lotto, L. S. and Astuto, T. A. (1984) 'Effective schools and school improvement: A comparative analysis of two lines of inquiry'. *Educational Administration Quarterly*, **20** (3), 41–68.

Cohen, L. and Manion, L. (1985) *Research Methods in Education*. London: Croom Helm.

Coopers and Lybrand (1988) *Local Management of Schools*. London: Coopers and Lybrand.

Cumming, J. (1986) *Evaluating your own school: a guide to action*. Victoria, NSW: Victoria Institute of Education.

Croll, P. (1986) *Systematic Classroom Observation*. London: Falmer Press.

Davies, B. (1989) 'Economics and Budgeting, in Fidler, B. and Bowles, G. (eds) (see below).

Dean, J. (1985) *Managing the Secondary School*. London: Croom Helm.

Delamont, S. (1983) *Interaction in the Classroom*. London: Methuen.

DeRoche, E. F. (1981) *An Administrator's Guide for Evaluating Programs and Personnel*. Boston: Allyn and Bacon.

Drucker, P. F. (1955) *The Practice of Management*. London: Heinemann.

Elliott, J. (1981) *Action Research: A Framework for Self Evaluation in Schools*. Cambridge: Cambridge Institute of Education, mimeo.

Elliott-Kemp, J. and Williams, G. L. (1980) *The DION Handbook*. Sheffield: Pavic Publications.

Everard, K. B. and Morris, G. (1985) *Effective School Management*. London: Harper and Row.

Fayol, H. (1916) 'Administration, Industrielle et Generale', quoted in Pollard, H. R. (1974) *Developments in Management Thought*. London: Heinemann.

Fidler, R. (1989) 'Background to the Education Reform Act', in Fidler, B. and Bowles, G. (eds) *Effective Local Management of Schools*. Harlow: BEMAS/Longman.

Fiedler, F. E. (1967) *A Theory of Leadership Effectiveness*. New York: McGraw-Hill.

Flanders, N. (1970) *Analysing Teaching Behaviour*. New York: Addison Wesley.

Fullan, M. (1982) *The Meaning of Educational Change*. New York: Teachers College Press.

Fullan, M. and Park, P. (1981) *Curriculum Implementation*. Toronto: Ministry of Education.

Galton, M. (1978) *British Mirrors*. Leicester: School of Education, Leicester University.

Gitlin, A. D. (1987) 'Common school structures and teacher behaviour', in Smyth, J. (ed) *Educating Teachers: Changing the Nature of Pedagogical Knowledge*. London: Falmer.

Goetz, J. P. and LeCompte, M. D. (1984) *Ethnography and Qualitative Design in Educational Research*. New York: Academic Press.

Gray, H. L. (ed) (1988) *Management Consultancy in Schools*. London: Cassell.

Handy, C. and Aitken, R. (1986) *Understanding Schools as Organisations*. Harmondsworth: Penguin Books.

Hargreaves, D. H. *et al.* (1989) *Planning for School Development*. London: HMSO.

Harrison, E. F. (1978) *Management and Organisations*. Boston: Houghton Mifflin Co.

Hartnett, A. and Naish, M. (1990) 'The sleep of reason breeds monsters: the birth of a statutory curriculum in England and Wales'. *Journal of Curriculum Studies*, 22 (1), 1–16.

Hastings, C. *et al.* (1986) *The Superteam Solution*. Aldershot: Gower.

HMI/Scottish Education Department (1988) *Effective Primary Schools*. London: HMSO.

HMI/Scottish Education Department (1988) *Effective Secondary Schools*. London: HMSO.

Hersey, P. and Blanchard, K. H. (1972) *Management of Organizational Behaviour*. Englewood Cliffs, NJ: Prentice-Hall.

Herzberg, F. (1966) *Work and the Nature of Man*. Cleveland: World Publishing Co.

Hicks, H. G. (1972) *The Management of Organizations: A Systems and Human Resources Approach*. New York: McGraw-Hill.

Hill, D. (1988) 'An LEA Perspective from Cambridgeshire', in Oldroyd, D. and Caldwell, B. J. (eds) *Local Financial Management and the Self Managing School*. Bristol: National Development Centre for School Management Training.

Holmes, M. and Wynne, E. A. (1989) *Making the School an Effective Community*. London: Falmer Press.

Holroyde, G. (1976) 'Effective Management', in Macbeath, J. *A Question of Schooling*. London: Hodder and Stoughton.

Hook, C. (1981) *Studying Classrooms*. Victoria: Deakin University Press.

Hopkins, D. (1985) *A Teacher's Guide to Classroom Research*. Milton Keynes: Open University.

Hopkins, D. (1988) *Doing School Based Review: Instruments and Guidelines*. Leuven, Belgium: ACCO.

Hopkins, D. (1989) *Evaluation for School Development*. Milton Keynes: Open University.

House of Commons (1980) *Education Act 1980*. London: HMSO.

House of Commons (1986) *Education (no 2) Act 1986*. London: HMSO.

House of Commons (1988) *Education Reform Act 1988*. London: HMSO.

Huberman, A. M. and Miles, M. B. (1984) *Innovation Up Close: How School Improvement Works*. New York: Plenum.

Iano, R. P. (1986) 'The study and development of teaching: with implications for the advancement of special education'. *Remedial and Special Education*, **7** (5), 50–61.

Jesson, D. and Mayston, D. (1990) 'Information, accountability and educational performance indicators', in Fitz-Gibbon, C. T. (ed) *Performance Indicators*. Cleveden: Multilingual Matters.

Johnson, D. W. and Johnson, F. P. (1982) *Joining Together*. Englewood Cliffs: Prentice-Hall.

Johnson, D. W. and Johnson, R. T. (1989) *Leading the Cooperative School*. Edina: Interaction Book Co.

Jones, A. (1987) *Leadership for Tomorrow's Schools*. Oxford: Basil Blackwell.

Joyce, B. and Showers, B. (1988) *Student Achievement Through Staff Development*. London: Longman.

Lewin, K. (1951). *Field Theory in Social Science*. New York: Harper and Row.

Likert, R. (1967) *The Human Organization*. New York: McGraw-Hill.

Lincoln, Y. S. and Guba, E. G. *Naturalistic Inquiry*. Beverly Hills: Sage.

McAlister, D. and Connolly, M. (1990) 'Local Financial Management', in Cave, E. and Wilkinson, C. (eds) (see above).

McClelland, D. (1961) *The Achieving Society*. Princeton: Van Nostrand.

McGregor, D. (1960) *The Human Side of Enterprise*. New York: McGraw-Hill.

McMahon, A. *et al.* (1984) *The Grids Primary School Handbook* and *The Grids Secondary School Handbook*. York: Longman.

Maslow, A. (1954) *Motivation and Personality*. London: Harper and Row.

Miles, M. B. (1979) 'Qualitative data as an attractive nuisance: The problem of analysis'. *Administrative Science Quarterly*, **24** (4), 590–601.

Miles, M. B. (1981) *Learning to work in Groups*. New York: Teachers' College Press.

Miles, M. B. and Huberman, A. M. (1984) *Qualitative Data Analysis: A Source Book of New Methods*. London: Sage.

Millman, J. (ed) (1981) *Handbook of Teacher Evaluation*. Beverly Hills: Sage Publications.

Mintzberg, H. (1979) *The Structuring of Organizations*. Englewood Cliffs: Prentice-Hall.

Mortimore, P. *et al.* (1989) *School Matters - The Junior Years*. Exeter: Open Books.

National Curriculum Council (1990) *The Whole Curriculum*. London: HMSO.

National Steering Group for Teacher Appraisal (1989) *School Teacher Appraisal - A National Framework*. London: HMSO.

Open University (1981) *Course E364: Curriculum Evaluation and Assessment*. Milton Keynes: Open University Press.

Oxfordshire Education Department (1979) *Starting Points in Self Evaluation*. Oxford: Oxford County Council.

Pearce, J. (1986) *Standards and the LEA - The Accountability of Schools*. Windsor: NFER-Nelson.

Pemberton, M. (1982) *A Guide to Effective Meetings*. London: The Industrial Society.

Peters, T. J. and Waterman, R. H. (1982) *In Search of Excellence: Lessons from America's Best Run Companies*. London: Harper and Row.

Powney, J. and Watts, M. (1987) *Interviewing in Educational Research*. London: Routledge.

Rackham, N., Honey, P. and Colbert, M. (eds) (1971) *Developing Interactive Skills*. Northampton: Wellens.

Rosenshine, B. (1983) 'Teacher functions in instructional programmes'. *The Elementary School Journal*, **83**, 335–351.

Rutter, M. *et al.* (1979) *Fifteen Thousand Hours*. London: Open Books.

Schmuck, R. A. and Runkel, P. J. (1985) *The Handbook of Organizational Development in Schools*. Palo Alto, CA: Mayfield.

Schon, D. (1983) *The Reflective Practitioner*. New York: Basic Books.

Sexton, S. (1988) *Our Schools - A Radical Policy*. London: ILEA (Education Unit).

Simkins, T. and Lancaster, D. (1987) *Budgeting and Resource Allocation in Educational Institutions*. Sheffield: Sheffield City Polytechnic.

Skrtic, T. M. (1985) 'Doing naturalistic research into educational organisation', in Lincoln, Y. S. *Organizational Theory and Inquiry*. Beverly Hills: Sage.

Skrtic, T. M. (1988) 'The organisational context of special education', in Meyen, E. L. and Skrtic, T. M. (eds) *Exceptional Children and Youth: An Introduction*. Denver: Love.

Spradley, J. P. (1979) *The Ethnographic Interview*. New York: Holt, Rinehart and Winston.

Steers, R. M. and Porter, L. W. (1983) *Motivation and Work Behaviour*. New York: McGraw-Hill.

Stenhouse, L. (1975) *An Introduction to Curriculum Research and Development*. London: Heinemann.

Stewart, J. D. (1974) *The Responsive Local Authority*. London: Charles Knight.

Stillman, A. and Grant, M. (1989) *The LEA Adviser - A Changing Role*. Windsor: NFER-Nelson.

Stogdill, R. M. (1974) *Handbook of Leadership: A Survey of Theory and Research*. New York: Free Press.

Styan, D. *et al.* (1990) *Developing School Management: The way forward* (Report by the School Management Task Force). London: HMSO.

Taylor, W. (1976) 'The Head as Manager: Some Criticisms', in Peters, R. S. (ed) *The Role of the Head*. London: Routledge, Kegan Paul.

Terry, G. R. (1972) *Principles of Management*. Illinois: Richard Irwin.

Thomas, G. (1988) 'LFM in a Secondary School', in Downes, P. (ed) *Local Financial Management in Schools*. Oxford: Basil Blackwell.

Torrington, D. and Weightman, J. (1989) *The Reality of School Management*. Oxford: Basil Blackwell.

Walker, R. (1985) *Doing Research: A Handbook for Teachers*. London: Routledge.

Warwick, D. (1982) *Effective Meetings*. London: The Industrial Society.

Watts, P. (1983) *A Study of Alternative Frameworks in School Science*. Unpublished PhD Thesis. Surrey: University of Surrey.

West, M. and Bollington, R. (1990) *Teacher Appraisal: A practical guide for schools*. London: David Fulton.

Whitaker, P. (1983) *The Primary Head*. London: Heinemann.

Winkley, D. (1985) *Diplomats and Detectives: LEA Advisers at Work*. London: Robert Royce.

Woods, P. (1986) *Inside Schools*. London: Routledge.

Wragg, E. C. (1980) *Conducting and Analysing Interviews* (Rediguide 11). Nottingham: School of Education, University of Nottingham.

Youngman, M. B. (1986) *Analysing Questionnaires*. Nottingham: School of Education, University of Nottingham.

Yukl, G. A. (1981) *Leadership in Organizations*. Englewood Cliffs, NJ: Prentice-Hall.

Index of Key Points